Sir Albert Richardson
1880–1964

Alan Powers *editor*
Simon Houfe · John Wilton-Ely

SIR ALBERT RICHARDSON 1880–1964

HEINZ GALLERY
1999

Published on the occasion
of the exhibition *Sir Albert Richardson* at the
RIBA Heinz Gallery, 21 Portman Square, London W1
9 September–23 October, 1999

ISBN 1 872911 95 1

Heinz Gallery, 21 Portman Square, London W1H 9HF
Orders after May 2000 should be sent to RIBA Bookshop
66 Portland Place, London W1N 4DS

Designed by Dalrymple
Typeset in Monotype Columbus
Printed by BAS Printers Ltd

Cover: Leith House, Gresham Street, London, 1925–6
perspective by J.D.M. Harvey, 1924

Opposite title page *figure 1*
Photograph of Sir Albert Richardson in his
London office, *c.*1950

Contents

ACKNOWLEDGEMENTS

We particularly wish to thank the sponsors of the exhibition, the Whitbread Trusts and the Delafield Fund, and acknowledge the continuing support of the Drue Heinz Trust. The exhibition has been curated by Alan Powers, to whom we are profoundly grateful. Simon Houfe, Albert Richardson's grandson, has been the principal lender and without his work and willing cooperation the exhibition could not have happened. Other lenders to whom we are grateful are the Master and Fellows of Gonville & Caius College, Cambridge, Mr S.P.A. Holland, the Art Workers Guild, the Guild of Incorporated Surveyors, the Royal Academy of Arts, and the PCC of St Michael & All Angels, Millbrook. CH

As curator and editor, I would like to thank Simon Houfe, John Wilton-Ely, James Collett-White and the staff of the Bedfordshire County Record Office, Simon Bradley, Elain Harwood, Richard Ivey, Peter Smithson, Nick Savage (Royal Academy Library), Jeff Walden (BBC Written Archives Centre), Carolyn Watkins for loan of a copy of her Diploma thesis on Richardson at Thames Polytechnic, 1987, Denny Wickham, and the staff of the RIBA Drawings Collection and Library. AP

figure 2
Candelabrum for Merchant Taylors Hall (detail), *c.*1956

Foreword

I first encountered the work of Sir Albert Richardson when, as a new boy at the Company's school, I was taken up to London to the Livery Hall of the Worshipful Company of Merchant Taylors. There we were each given booklets about the history of the Company and its buildings. Within the shell of the 14th-century hall, rebuilt after the Great Fire and again gutted in 1941, Richardson created a rich and appropriate setting for one of the Great Twelve Livery Companies, described rather unflatteringly in the latest Pevsner as 'unashamedly backward-looking, though redeemed somewhat by impeccable craftsmanship'. Responding to the layers of history represented by the building (literally in that a trapdoor under the carpet reveals earlier floors of the 14th century, 1646 and 1675), Richardson added a further layer that is unmistakably of its period (completed 1959) but sympathetic to the building's complex past.

In many ways, Merchant Taylors Hall sums up Richardson as an architect. He had an immense respect for the work of past generations, particularly those of the 18th and early 19th centuries but he was no slavish copyist. His huge bronze chandeliers for the Merchant Taylors betray the influence of the Regency collector and designer Thomas Hope, some of whose furniture he owned, yet the results could never have been designed by Hope. They represent a valid view of classicism carried forward and redefined for the mid-20th century, examples of his dictum that 'intelligent evolution is the true meaning of modernity'. Yet long before his death in 1964 he had already become a dinosaur to the younger members of his profession, dismissed as an eccentric who could only appeal to clients of a similar age. The unjustness of this verdict is indicated by the official recognition of the importance of Bracken House, Cannon St, London (1955–59), which in 1987 became the first post-war building to be listed.

Richardson's interest in architecture was broad. He was a prolific author whose books show as voracious an interest in the design solutions of anonymous Regency country builders as the leaders of the profession such as Henry Holland, whom he particularly revered. His *Monumental Classic Architecture in Great Britain and Ireland* (1914) was a pioneering study that brought back to public notice the work of forgotten architects such as Cuthbert Brodrick, Charles Robert Cockerell and Alexander Thomson. He built up a truly remarkable collection of historic architectural drawings, unfortunately dispersed in 1983, which he viewed as a working tool as much as fine art and he was remembered as a generous teacher at the Bartlett School.

A full architectural biography of Richardson remains to be written, for the excellent biography by his grandson Simon Houfe, published in 1980, is a personal memoir rather than a discussion of his work. The documentation on Richardson's career is very extensive, with a quantity of Richardson & Gill drawings in the RIBA but the huge majority on deposit in the Bedfordshire County Record Office, an appropriate location for the work of a man who so strongly identified with his adopted county. This exhibition, the 152nd and final one to be held in the RIBA Heinz Gallery, will, we hope, go far to re-establish Richardson's position as a significant figure in the 20th century history of British architecture and reawaken interest in his work.

Charles Hind *Curator, The British Architectural Library Drawings Collection*

MONUMENTAL CLASSIC ARCHITECTURE IN GREAT BRITAIN AND IRELAND DURING THE XVIIIth & XIXth CENTURIES

A. E. RICHARDSON

'A vindication of classical principles': Albert Richardson and his historical sources

JOHN WILTON-ELY

When it appeared in 1914, Albert Richardson's *Monumental Classic Architecture in Great Britain and Ireland during the 18th and 19th centuries* represented a landmark not only in the historiography of British architectural history but in the attitude towards the inspiration of the past for contemporary designers. Had it not been for the social and economic changes following the First World War, the general impact of this seminal publication would probably have been more profound but its prime concerns were to have a lasting consequence on Richardson's own work as an inspiring teacher, designer and restorer. As David Watkin observed, referring to this magisterial book: 'The whole picture of English architecture so carefully built up by Blomfield and his contemporaries was now reversed as a mirror-image, so that the period they had most despised, the later eighteenth and early nineteenth centuries, was seen as the triumphant climax of the movement begun by Inigo Jones. According to this new assessment, the grand tradition of buildings represented by the work of C.R. Cockerell, H.L. Elmes, James Pennethorne and Alexander Thomson had been wantonly destroyed by the nationalism of the Gothic Revival and of the Arts and Crafts Movement, so that it was left to Richardson and his generation to pick up the pieces and build a new and glorious classical future. Where his immediate predecessors and indeed, many of his contemporaries, had been nationalist, Richardson was cosmopolitan so that he was able to refer with knowledgeable enthusiasm to the torch of classicism as kept alight by Joseph Louis Duc, Jacques Ignace Hittorf and Henri Labrouste in France, by Karl Friedrich Schinkel in Germany, and in his own day, by McKim, Mead and White in North America.'[1]

opposite · figure 3
Monumental Classic Architecture, 1914, binding design by Percy Delf Smith

above · figure 4
C.R. Cockerell (1788–1863), Bank of England, Liverpool, 1845, photo by E. Dockree

Although never a revivalist, as he has frequently been portrayed, Richardson followed Sir Joshua Reynolds in the conviction that regular contact with the achievements of the classical past was an enlivening and inspirational source for contemporary expression.[2] Now that the achievements of the Modern Movement can be viewed more dispassionately, this has been found to be equally true, if less explicit, of such radical designers as Le Corbusier, Walter Gropius and Ludwig Mies van der Rohe. Throughout Richardson's writings, lectures and public statements over some 50 years, this belief in the fundamental principles and humanism of classicism never deserted him. Moreover, those students of the Georgian achievement, such as the present writer, who greatly benefited from personal contact with him during his last years, have seen his ideals recognised and vindicated within the past two decades as an overt expression of Classicism has re-entered the field of contemporary design, even if often lacking the discriminating and scholarly principles on which Richardson founded his work. Moreover, many of the British classical architects and designers of the late 18th and 19th centuries whom he championed almost single-handed in the early decades of this century are now universally admired and are subjects of substantial monographs, exhibitions and continuing research.[3]

Richardson's training and work in the offices of Hellicar, Stokes and Verity gave him an unusual combination of formal attitudes towards design which appeared early in his scholarly writings and publications.[4] From the Arts and Crafts preoccupations of the first two masters, he learnt the value of traditional materials and qualities of craftsmanship within the vernacular and regional traditions in British architecture, without being affected by the associational and sentimental which often typified that late 19th-century word. From Verity, on the other hand, he rapidly enlarged his formal horizons in terms of an international classicism, represented by the Ecole des Beaux-Arts, which employed the new steel and concrete technology, even if he was not entirely won over by the latter as a direct material means of expression. His facade of the Central London Polytechnic in Upper Regent Street, which he designed in 1907, shows a remarkable assimilation of the formal system and vocabulary of the Beaux-Arts school in marked contrast to the banal classicism of surrounding facades in Upper Regent Street.

figure 5
Representative Balcony Railings, from *London Houses 1660–1830*, 1911

Predictably, Richardson was a leading figure among the circle of architects, led by S.D. Adshead, who set up the short-lived Classical Society in 1908. While the English Renaissance and Wren had been imaginatively interpreted by Shaw and his contemporaries during the last decades of the previous century, later designers in the classical tradition, British as well as Continental, had largely been ignored by the architectural profession as well as by scholarship in general. The Society, which included Charles Reilly, Edwin Cooper, Vincent Harris, John Anderson and Lutyens, among others, saw Classicism as offering a coherent and challenging system of design principles. By reacting against the romanticism and individualism of Shaw's generation, they sought to return to the historic tradition of western architecture which Britain was thought to have discarded with the 19th-century Gothic revival.[5] French classical discipline in design, enshrined in the Ecole des Beaux-Arts, was regarded as providing a model for the reform of architectural education while the contemporary work of McKim, Mead and White in America was seen as confirming the vital modernity of classicism and the compatibility of its aesthetic principles with steel-framed structures. As the member of the Classical Society who published extensively, Richardson's personal commitment to late 18th and 19th-century continental classicism was manifested by a series of pioneering articles in the *Architectural Review* from 1911 onwards which included 'The Style Neo-Grec', 'The Empire Style in England', 'Jean Charles Krafft, Architecte-Dessinateur', 'Karl Friedrich Schinkel', 'Classic Architecture in Russia', 'Jacques Ignace Hittorf' and 'The Palais de Justice, Paris, and its remodelling by Joseph Louis Duc'.[6]

Ever the teacher, Richardson demonstrated his belief in the continuing relevance of classical exemplars in his first book, *London Houses from 1660 to 1820. A Consideration of their Architecture and Detail*, which was jointly produced with his partner Charles Lovett Gill and published by Herbert Batsford in 1911. It is typical of the man that he could swiftly move from the monumental international classicism of France, Germany and Russia, as well as the sophisticated Regency interiors of Thomas Hope, to the intimate scale and mundane brick architecture of late Stuart and Georgian speculators in squares and terrace housing. His main objective was to reveal the same classic principles operating in a living tradition, traced from the periods of Jones and Wren to those of Adam and Soane. The didactic function of this elegantly produced book is clearly stated in the Preface as 'primarily intended for the study of architects either practising in, or visiting the Metropolis; and not only will its purpose appeal to English or Colonial Architects, but also to those of other nationalities; because the London House contains features, which as motifs for transposition, are universally applauded'.[7] At this time the London squares in particular, which were still largely intact and unaffected by unsympathetic development, were barely regarded as serious subjects of study, and the fine plate photographs specially taken by A.E. Walsham (apart from a few interiors by Bedford Lemere & Co.) which augment the 18th-century views of the urban spaces, make nostalgic viewing today. The short introductory text ranges from a discussion of planning, room proportions and interior decoration to the discussion of the handling of materials and fittings, such as fanlights, glazing bars, and doorcases, as well as the treatment of ironwork in balustrades, railings and balconies. The setting of the individual buildings within the urban space concerned is also given emphasis in a commentary taking the form of detailed notes which accompany each illustration.

During Richardson's early travels throughout this country and the Continent, especially in France, he was tirelessly accumulating a large quantity of sketches and analytical studies of architecture which enabled him to judge the distinctive character of the British classical achievement within a wider context. He was increasingly convinced of the lessons to be learnt from the eclectic and finely-enriched system of design found in architects as diverse as Schinkel, Klenze, Duc, Hittorf and Labrouste. This system was characterised by its combination of the formal astringency of Greek classicism with the experimental tradition and ornamental richness of late Roman and Italian Renaissance design – a creative synthesis which, for him, was to be the essence of the Neo-Grec style and absorbed into his own designs. In terms of the British achievement, this was to lead him towards an unqualified admiration for the neglected designers of Victorian classicism, notably C.R. Cockerell and Harvey Lonsdale Elmes. Such sources provided the inspiration for Richardson's first major design – the New Theatre (later Opera House) at Manchester, completed in 1912, with a composition showing an exceptionally accomplished command of ornamental forms within a finely proportioned structure of marked restraint. In the preliminary designs for the principal facade, which reveal the marked influence of his admired continental exemplars in 19th-century French classicism, it is the final act of inserting the arched feature within the tympanum in the executed building which reveals Richardson's clear understanding of Cockerell's distinctive application of the classical canon, particularly as found in his Bank of England, Liverpool. As Charles Reilly observed, when writing about Richardson's theatre in a survey of Manchester buildings in 1924, 'what makes this exterior so striking and so different to that of any other theatre or cinema I know is the simplicity and strength of its main lines. The building is sufficiently rhetorical for its purpose yet remains in essence dignified and simple'.[8]

figure 6
Balcony in Euston Square, from *London Houses 1660–1830*, 1911

figure 7
Richardson & Gill with Horace Farquharson, New Theatre, Manchester, 1912 (drawing by Hanslip Fletcher)

In 1913 Richardson delivered a series of lectures at University College, London, on 'The Work of the English Architects of the Eighteenth Century and Neo-Classic School of the Nineteenth Century', sponsored by the Carpenters Company, which were subsequently published in the *Architects' and Builders' Journal*. This material was expanded to form the text of the exceptionally lavish treatise *Monumental Classic Architecture*, commissioned by Batsford and published the following year with a dedication to the Prince of Wales. As with his book on London houses, he was concerned to encourage creative reform by a survey of striking examples and in this case Richardson aimed to promote a greater concern for academic discipline in urban design, strongly inspired by the French tradition. Here he broke new ground by drawing attention to the great and largely neglected achievement of public architecture in Britain and Ireland from its genesis under Inigo Jones to the triumphant climax in the middle of the 19th century. As he expressed it in the Preface: 'An academic style is necessary to the architecture of great civic centres: without its benign and uplifting influence the correct tone of the capital can never be obtained. All building partakes somewhat of this character which prevails at such culminating points of interest. Where else is it to obtain its impression? What else exists to be mirrored? When the tone at the centre of the city is decadent there concurs a corresponding depression on the outskirts.'[9]

figure 8
Richardson delivering the Carpenters Company lectures in 1913

As with many of his later books, Richardson took considerable care over the design and presentation of the volume, from the finely embossed cover and spine down to the careful juxtaposition of images on the page openings. His visual material was carefully selected to reinforce his views, and the sheer wealth of outstanding plate photographs (many of them in exceptionally impressive collotype images), accompanied by measured plans, sections and elevations by colleagues and students, gave this work a formidable sense of authority.[10] While the argument was thus presented in a strongly visual manner, somewhat reminiscent of Richardson's flamboyant lecturing manner, the circuitous text is couched in an appropriately sonorous style which, as often in his later writings, is inclined to digress and occasionally to fall into lists of works. There are, however, a number of memorable passages possessing an almost Johnsonian rhetoric, as appropriate to such a manifesto. For instance, referring to George Dance's Newgate Prison, he writes: 'Real architecture requires to be moulten in the imagination of the designer; to be ready as it were to emerge from such a crucible in one instantaneous gush. Then it attains to such power and significance as to leave an impression, on the mind of all beholders, of a perfect coherent and indivisible whole.'[11]

figure 9
Sir John Soane (1753–1837), Bank of England, 1804–7, photo by E. Dockree

opposite · figure 10
'A Small Shop Window at Edmonton', drawing by G. Grey Wornum, from *The Smaller English House*, 1925

The book divides the rise of monumental design into four phases, beginning with Roman Palladianism (1730–80) in which the unrivalled range of surviving public buildings in Dublin by James Gandon and Thomas Cooley were celebrated, together with William Chambers's Somerset House and Dance's Newgate. This was followed by the Graeco-Roman phase (1780–1820) where the Greek Revival, pioneered by James 'Athenian' Stuart and the scholarly circle of the Society of Dilettanti, was shown to combine with Roman classicism in John Soane – the ideal professional academic architect – particularly in the creation of the Bank of England. Here, as if forming an architectural elegy, are photographs of Soane's masterpiece, together with John Nash's Regent Street and John Rennie's Blackfriars Bridge – all to be swept away within the next thirty years.[12] If an evaluation of Soane and Nash was a work of pioneering scholarship at the time, even more so was Richardson's treatment of the designers of his 'Greek Phase' (1820–40); in particular, William Wilkins, Robert Smirke, William Henry Playfair and Thomas Hamilton. Finally, the culmination of the monumental tradition, as he saw it, in two parallel if interrelated movements – the Neo-Grec and the Italian phase – was all the more remarkable at a time when the last of the

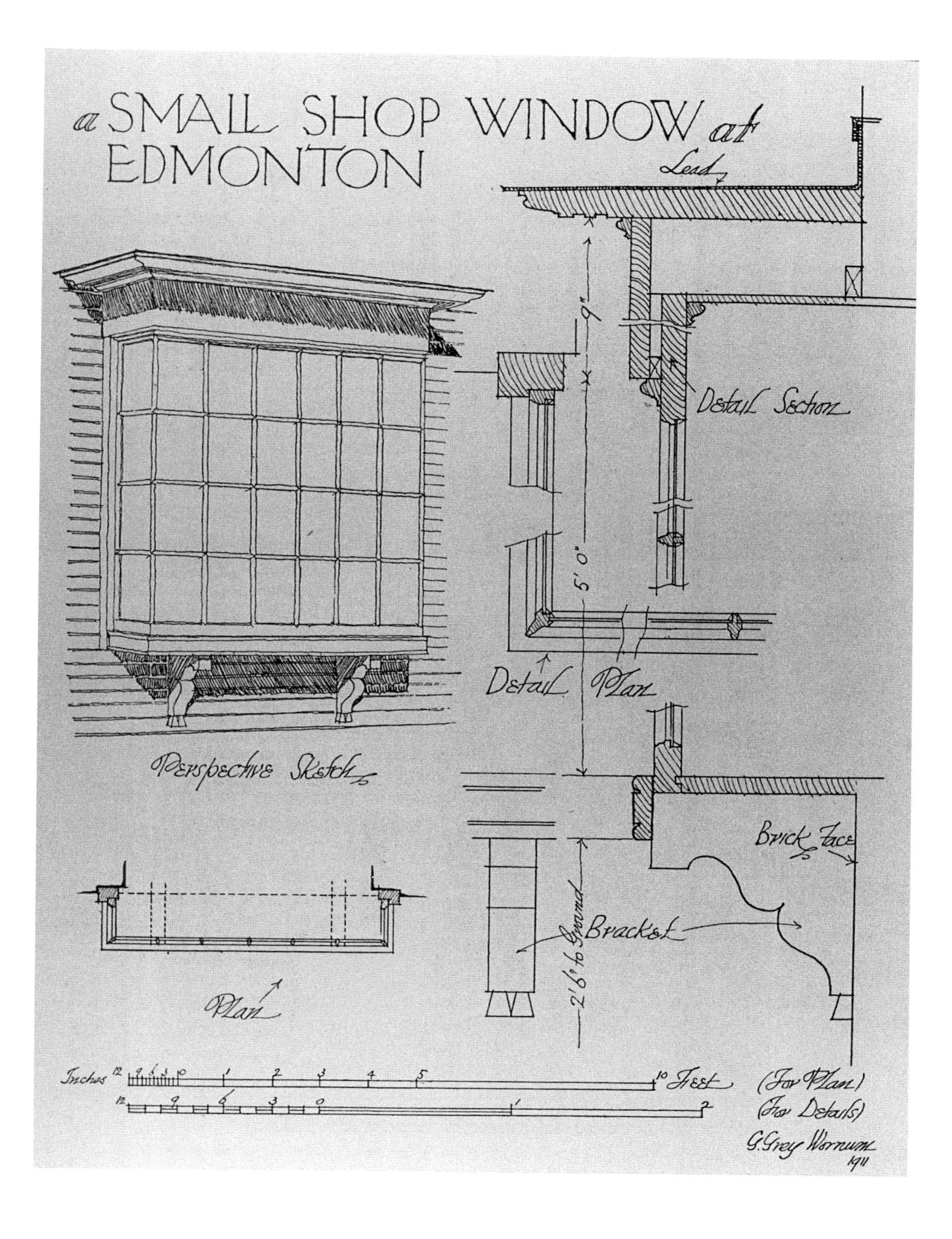
a SMALL SHOP WINDOW at
EDMONTON
Lead
9"
Detail Section
5' 0"
Detail Plan
Perspective Sketch
Brick Face
Bracket
2' 6" to Ground
Plan
Inches 12 9 6 3 0 1 2 3 4 5 10 Feet (For Plan)
12 9 6 3 0 1 2 (For Details)
G. Grey Wornum
1911

major architects examined, Alexander 'Greek' Thomson, had died only five years before Richardson's birth and the last work illustrated – the Harris Library, Preston, by James Hibbert – was finished in 1896 as he was beginning his tutelage under Frank Page. Characterising this final phase, Richardson discerned 'something of the Homeric age, something eloquent of the idyllic Italian Renaissance, and moreover, something essentially modern'.[13] For him the heroes of this triumphant synthesis of the Greek and Roman legacies of achievement were to be C.R. Cockerell, Harvey Lonsdale Elmes and Charles Barry who, 'while they demonstrated the suitability of the Hellenic motif, avoided the pedantic reproduction of its forms. They viewed the architectural problems of their day with the eyes of Greeks, full of appreciation for the purest sensuous beauty, never overstepping

figure 11
Lodge at Princetown, from *Regional Architecture in the West of England*, 1924

figure 12
John Foulston (1772–1842), St Michael's Terrace, Stoke Damerel, Devon, *c.*1825, from *Regional Architecture in the West of England*, 1924

the limits of the academic, and thoroughly understanding the impartation of correct architectural character.'[14]

This value of the academic was of central concern throughout Richardson's thought and writings during these years, particularly since he had worked in two offices where the benefits of a coherent system of institutional training, offsetting the individualistic tradition of British architecture at the turn of the century, were fully recognised. Stokes as a former president of the Architectural Association (1888–91) had been involved in the movement away from articled pupilage towards systematic instruction in full-time schools of architecture, while Verity's career and outlook embodied the values of the structured training within a core philosophy of design at the Ecole des Beaux-Arts. Richardson had already presented these views in a paper, 'The Academic in Architecture', delivered at the RIBA in 1912, in which he said: 'Contrary to prevalent opinion, originality and individuality do play a part in the development of the academic; as component attributes their presence is inevitable and welcome. The inventive faculty is strengthened by contact with tradition; the old truths and beauties are brought out again in stronger relief and are displayed in the garb of modernity.'[15] It was to be a natural move in his career, therefore, when he was appointed to succeed F.M. Simpson in the Chair of Architecture at the Bartlett School of London University in 1919.

Apart from a growing number of new professional responsibilities, the demanding tasks of teaching and of running an institution such as the Bartlett School absorbed a great deal of Richardson's creative energies over these years. His views continued to be as effective in conditioning the development of architectural history as much as that of the creative discipline. For example, the impact and idiosyncratic style of his methods of communicating the relevance of the classical past to students made a lasting impression on Sir John Summerson who was among the new intake of 1922. As he recalled some 58 years later, Richardson 'was the first architect and architectural historian I ever met, also the first enthusiast, and I found him kind but alarming. Then in his early forties, he seemed in a state of perpetual motion, bowling through the studios, lecturing against the clock with prophetic urgency, exhorting us to attend, before it was too late, to the massive power of hypostyle halls, the structural grandeur of aqueducts or what he liked to call the "nervous artistry" of antique ornament.... We mocked him a little but we were impressed and the reason for that was that whether he was talking about Assyrian or Egyptian or Greek or Roman or Georgian or his beloved Cockerell, he was talking about one thing; just simply architecture, ageless and sublime'.[16]

Throughout his career, Richardson's professional commissions tended to divide broadly between urban and sophisticated monumental designs on the one hand and modest regional works, reflecting local vernacular traditions and materials, on the other. As already shown, quite early on his enthusiasms and scholarship also represented this range in treatment from his discussion of major complexes, such as Somerset House or the Bank of England, to his analysis of modest but well-designed anonymous terraces and villas in Georgian London. Although introduced in his London book, his first really extensive treatment of classicism at work in this latter field appeared in 1924 with *Regional Architecture in the West of England,* produced in collaboration with Gill (whose main contribution consisted of the photographs) and dedicated to Edward, Duke of Cornwall. Again, the resulting book was intended to have a practical purpose for contemporary designers. As the Preface states: 'At this present attempts are being made throughout the country to re-establish a form of building expression which has the merit of being traditional; it is essential, therefore, in this study to take into account conditions that formerly pertained, such as local trading interests, available materials, the proximity of large towns, the existence of trunk roads, the navigable rivers and canals and other factors, all of which played a part in determining contemporary prosperity.'[17] Similar in approach to their first book on the London house, the authors applied a chronological approach in three phases, concentrating on the expression of vernacular as well as sophisticated classicism from 1730 to 1850. Separate chapters on specific areas, including Exeter, Plymouth and the Isles of Scilly, served to demonstrate classicism at work in particular locations as applied to a hierarchy of building types from farms to villas and banks to customs houses. No detail was too small to make the point as a plate of comparative door-knockers demonstrates.

figure 13
Houses in Hugh Town, St Mary's, Scilly Isles, from *Regional Architecture in the West of England,* 1924

For the first time in one of Richardson's books, in addition to a plentiful quantity of prints, and photographs, he included a number of his own vivid thumbnail drawings selected from his sketch books. These brisk studies summed up with a masterly economy the essence of what he wished to communicate, rather in the fashion of his large-scale virtuoso sketches, dashed off in the heat of lecturing to his Bartlett students, or the ink drawings on glass lantern slides used for the same purpose. Demonstrating his instinctive feel for the life of classical forms, he was to retain this facility to the last years of his life when engaged in animated conversations, whether in his study, at the dinner table or autographing books. When schooling the present author in the hierarchy of the classical orders, Richardson at the drawing board in his early 80s was still capable of executing fine free-hand profiles of mouldings and details of ornamental vocabulary with an instinctive and unhesitating manner, invariably accompanied by a ceaseless commentary punctuated by emphatic gestures.

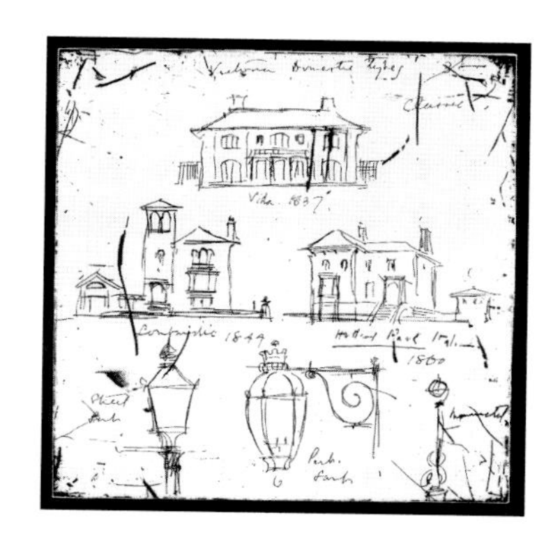

figure 14
'Victorian domestic types' (print from glass lecture slide drawn by Richardson)

In the same year that Richardson took over the Bartlett, he had finally acquired the much-desired house at Ampthill. Avenue House was to become in itself a source of inspiration, not only through the rapidly accumulating collections of art, furniture, books and drawings, but because it epitomised the kind of relatively modest late 18th-century house which he keenly admired in terms of its reticent, well proportioned spaces, lean classical mouldings and total fitness for purpose. Indeed on various occasions he referred to his new home as his 'yardstick and measuring scale'.[18] Some six years later, in 1925, this scale of building was to be the subject of a new book, *The Smaller English House of the Later Renaissance, 1660–1830. An Account of its Design, Plan and Details.* This was written in collaboration with the American writer H. Donaldson Eberlein, who had made an extensive study of classical colonial architecture in his own country and had been greatly inspired by Richardson's articles in the *Architect's Journal.*[19] It was to be another handsomely-produced book by Batsford and, like *Classic Monumental Architecture,* was also published in the United States. *The Smaller English House* covered another aspect of the English classical tradition; one which had largely been neglected in favour of the grander houses featured in Edward Hudson's *Country Life* and H. Avray Tipping's *English Homes.* Similar in approach and chronological limits to the London book of 1911, the intention was also to make available a wealth of classical concepts and details for the inspiration of contemporary designers. As also with the earlier surveys on London and the West Country, there was no intention to promote pastiche or 'Neo-Georgian'. (A term of opprobrium which Richardson regularly used to dismiss the illiterate and ubiquitous 'Georgian' public buildings and modern speculative homes which emerged between the Wars.) In their Preface the authors took pains to stress that 'it is not their desire to dogmatise on the merits of the style they describe, or to expect the examples to be used as motifs' but that they 'view the humane pleasantries of the features of the houses and the originality of the detail, apart from its classical tendencies, as offering ideas to architects and the public, which, besides having an historical interest, will form a standard of good taste and proportion'.[20] Apart from photographs (including three of Avenue House), many taken by Eberlein, and a wealth of Richardson's vivid sketches and summary plans, the illustrations also included a number of detailed measured drawings, made in 1911 by the architect Grey Wornum, serving to stress the careful attention to detail that characterised the Georgian achievement, even found among modest and 'anonymous' buildings throughout England. After a chronological sketch outlining domestic development from the Queen Anne House to the works of S.P. Cockerell, J.B. Papworth, John Nash and Decimus Burton, the remaining chapters were devoted to practical aspects of design: namely the 'Evolution of Plan'; 'Materials and Craftsmanship'; and 'Varieties in Composition'. In the last chapter, 'Conclusion and Modern Uses', while accepting the value of the classical concepts and proportions demonstrated from facade to glazing bar, Richardson's belief in the importance of learning from a detailed study of case histories over a period of development is summarised in the final phrase, 'intelligent evolution is the true meaning of modernity'.[21]

figure 15
'Shaped door heads', drawing by G. Grey Wornum, from *The Smaller English House,* 1925

figure 16
Sir John Soane (1753–1837), Veranda at Moggerhanger, Bedfordshire, 1809–11, from *The Smaller English House,* 1925

During these years, although disagreeing with many of the more radical concepts of the Modern Movement, Richardson was still prepared to see positive applications of the classical discipline within avant garde contemporary design as strikingly manifested in his own award-winning design for the Sanderson's wallpaper building in St Margaret's House, Wells Street, London, of 1930–32, with its restrained classical formula across a steel frame. As he put it during an RIBA discussion on 'Modernism in Architecture' in 1928: 'We have learned to simplify, to invent, to economise. We have learned to meet new conditions. Planning has shown us the lines on which the new art is likely to develop. Concrete has demonstrated new possibilities. The copy-book has been relegated to the architectural nursery. But we architects nevertheless still have a just pride in the past, a reasonable view of the present, and a keen desire to invent. In the works of Sullivan, Otto Wagner, Tony Garnier, etc., you will find a vindication of classical principles. These men have advanced the art.'[22]

Throughout the 1920s and 1930s Richardson was rapidly acquiring an outstanding collection of architectural drawings, particularly by designers within the golden age of classicism, as he regarded the period between 1760 and the mid-19th century. In this collecting activity, as with his writings, he was a considerable pioneer and benefited from the low prices. Sadly, however, very little documentation exists of sources or dates of acquisition for these drawings since he was primarily concerned with their practical value to him as a committed classical architect and teacher operating within a living tradition where ideas and concepts mattered far more than the niceties of art-historical significance.[23] In this respect it is particularly significant that these historic works were purchased with money from the practice and Richardson's vigorous use of them as a daily source

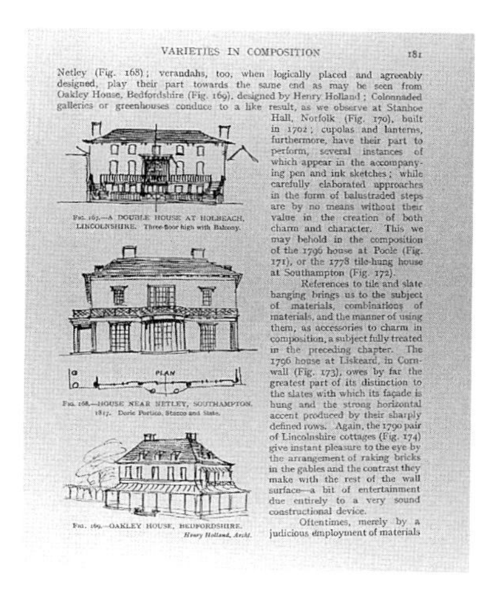
VARIETIES IN COMPOSITION 181

Netley (Fig. 168); verandahs, too, when logically placed and agreeably designed, play their part towards the same end as may be seen from Oakley House, Bedfordshire (Fig. 169), designed by Henry Holland; Colonnaded galleries or greenhouses conduce to a like result, as we observe at Stanhoe Hall, Norfolk (Fig. 170), built in 1702; cupolas and lanterns, furthermore, have their part to perform, several instances of which appear in the accompanying pen and ink sketches; while carefully elaborated approaches in the form of balustraded steps are by no means without their value in the creation of both charm and character. This we may behold in the composition of the 1796 house at Poole (Fig. 171), or the 1778 tile-hung house at Southampton (Fig. 172).

References to tile and slate hanging brings us to the subject of materials, combinations of materials, and the manner of using them, as accessories to charm in composition, a subject fully treated in the preceding chapter. The 1796 house at Liskeard, in Cornwall (Fig. 173), owes by far the greatest part of its distinction to the slates with which its façade is hung and the strong horizontal accent produced by their sharply defined rows. Again, the 1790 pair of Lincolnshire cottages (Fig. 174) give instant pleasure to the eye by the arrangement of raking bricks in the gables and the contrast they make with the rest of the wall surface—a bit of entertainment due entirely to a very sound constructional device.

Oftentimes, merely by a judicious employment of materials

FIG. 167.—A DOUBLE HOUSE AT HOLBEACH, LINCOLNSHIRE. Three-floor high with Balcony.

FIG. 168.—HOUSE NEAR NETLEY, SOUTHAMPTON. 1817. Doric Portico, Stucco and Slate.

FIG. 169.—OAKLEY HOUSE, BEDFORDSHIRE. Henry Holland, Archt.

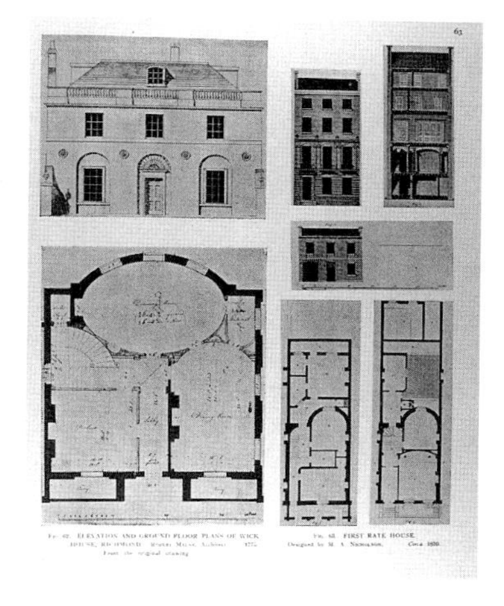

of inspiration was indicative of his wish to empathise with his predecessors. It is also symptomatic of this approach that few of the historic drawings were framed but kept in folios, both in London as well as Ampthill, where he was able to refer to them swiftly while designing as well as teaching. While there was a quantity of unidentified designs, predictably the roll-call of identified architects in the collection represented a continuity of classical experiment over a period of some 150 years which included Samuel Angell, Lancelot Brown (a group of designs for Peper Harrow), John Carr, William Chambers, C.R. Cockerell, J.M. Gandy, John Gibson, J.A. Hansom, Philip Hardwick, Thomas Harrison, David Laing, Robert Mylne, C.J. Richardson, Thomas Sandby, George Saunders, John Soane, Sir Robert Taylor, John Vardy, Lewis Vulliamy, and James and Samuel Wyatt.

This collection, which was largely dispersed in 1983, featured among its highlights an album containing well over one hundred designs by Robert Mylne, bought prior to 1925.[24] This exceptional group of designs, many of them executed in coloured washes with highly detailed technical information on roofing and drainage, indicated the deep respect with which Richardson regarded an architect whose instinctive feel for fine proportions and formal astringency, joined to sound construction and meticulous planning, characterised his own practice and teaching, In fact, his last book was to be *Robert Mylne, Architect and Engineer, 1733 to 1811*, published by Batsford in 1955. This latter publication noticeably suffered from having to be produced in the extremely demanding years as PRA and in the midst of a highly active post-war practice.[25] It nevertheless showed the insights that Richardson's own experience (which had included engineering training at the London Polytechnic and during the Great War) could throw on working procedures and practical concerns, as revealed in this transcription of Mylne's professional diary which covered almost his entire career between 1762 and 1810.

figure 17
'Varieties of Composition', drawing by Albert Richardson from *The Smaller English House*, 1925

figure 18
Sir William Chambers (1723–96), Library Ceiling at Woburn Abbey (drawing from Richardson's collection)

figure 19
Robert Mylne (1733–1811), Wick House, Richmond, original drawings from Richardson's collection, from *The Smaller English House*, 1925

In addition to an important collection of Chambers's business letters, a particularly seminal work in the collection was John Eastry Goodchild's scrap-book entitled *Reminiscences of my Twenty-Six years Association with Professor C.R. Cockerell.*[26] This latter covered virtually all of his commissions and projects from 1833 to 1859 and represented a major source of highly detailed information on Cockerell's activities as well as his artistic and intellectual development.[27] The 188 page album included drawings by the architect, engravings and photographs of buildings and autograph letters by the architect and his father, Samuel Pepys Cockerell. Like Chambers, Cockerell was to remain one of the leading exemplars to Richardson of a scholarly designer who engaged in an active professional life and showed the discerning and inventive application of classical principles from modest commissions to the highest expression of monumental buildings.

Reflecting his writings, the collection at Ampthill (as well as in his successive London offices) was also representative of Richardson's international range and wide terms of reference. Like Soane he firmly believed in the value of living within an environment where he was constantly surrounded by inspirational material, in terms both of drawings and of folios, engravings, models, casts and works of decorative arts as well as his own sketches, framed or accumulated in countless albums. Among his finest foreign drawings were works by Charles-Louis Clérisseau, Victor Louis and an exceptional group of highly finished designs by Giacomo Quarenghi which included the English Palace and landscape lay-out at Peterhof, the Alexander Palace at Tsarskoe Selo, and St George's Hall in the Winter Palace, St Petersburg. An impressive design for an illusionistic ceiling design, attributed to Andrea Pozzo, hung in his London office, while at Ampthill Giuseppe Vasi's vast engraved panorama of 18th-century Rome, as seen from the Janiculum, was accompanied on the walls by etchings from Piranesi's *Vedute di Roma*, together with prints of St Petersburg and Napoleon's Paris.

Richardson's extensive libraries of architectural folios and pattern books, both in Ampthill and London, were used in as thorough and robust a manner as by his 18th-century predecessors. In conversations during his later years, he repeatedly testified to the creative importance for him of engraved designs by Marot, Neufforge, Thomas Hope, Percier & Fontaine, and would think nothing of taking a taxi, in mid-conversation with the present writer in tow, to demonstrate an application from Neufforge on the facade of one of his London buildings.[28] A reference to these particular designers also underlines Richardson's lively response and comprehensive concern with interior design; Hope and Percier & Fontaine providing the same inspiration through their highly imaginative application of classical forms as found in Cockerell's works.[29] In fact Richardson's early

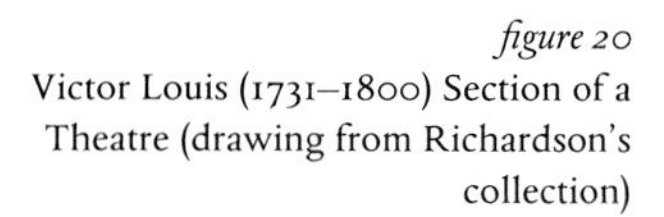

figure 20
Victor Louis (1731–1800) Section of a Theatre (drawing from Richardson's collection)

recognition of Hope's interior designs for his Duchess Street house in London through his 1911 articles on 'The Empire Style in England' and subsequent acquisition of pendant wall-lights by this designer (now in the Royal Pavilion, Brighton), was to play an important part in the Regency Revival in interior design and collecting after the First World War. Apart from furniture by Hope and Holland, he acquired drawings for decorative designs as widely ranging as a sketch for the painted scheme for the staircase ceiling at Grimsthorpe Castle by Sir James Thornhill and an exceptionally fine Chambers design for the Library ceiling at Woburn of 1767 to Alfred Stevens's lavish ornamental programme for Dorchester House, London, of 1856 and Edward Bell's opulent proposals for wall and ceiling decorations in the Octagon Room and Ball Room of the Bath Assembly Rooms of 1879 (the latter being restored by Richardson after the Second World War).[30]

The inter-war years marked a new phase in Richardson's literary and professional career as the brave promise of the new classicism began to fade and the more radical standpoint of the International Modern Movement became increasingly assertive in architectural thinking and education. New commercial pressures in development and urban expansion also began to threaten the classical heritage. In 1925 a second book was produced with Eberlein which examined another aspect of regional and provincial architecture where social history was reflected in vernacular as well as more sophisticated buildings, but subject to greater pressures for change. *The English Inn. Past and Present* recorded a remarkable range of buildings which were to be swiftly altered or drastically changed with the rapid advance of motor transport, although it is fair to say that Richardson himself was an enthusiastic user of the car and fully exploited the advantages it provided for rapid and exhaustive study tours as well as his professional duties. Since this book went swiftly out of print and more material was accumulated, Richardson published a further work alone on the same theme, *The Old Inns of England*, in 1934 with a cautionary Foreword by Lutyens referring to the 'regrettable exceptions, such as the adjectival "olde worlde" creations, which are as objectionable and as needless as are the ultra-modern, in that both deface our countryside'.[31] While the classical tradition was indicated in sophisticated examples, such as the Stamford Hotel, the White Hart at Salisbury and the Swan at Bedford, there are signs in both books of a growing nostalgia and retreat from the contemporary world which increasingly characterised Richardson's viewpoint and uses of the past as the inter-war years advanced. Gradually scholarship and practice were beginning to drift apart although moments of that creative synthesis which he deeply valued in Neo-Classicism continued to occur in his later work when provided with an exceptional challenge to relate new structures to an historic environment.

As a kind of valediction to the age which he most revered, Richardson's encyclopaedic *Georgian England: A Survey of Social Life, Trades, Industries & Art from 1700 to 1820*, published in 1931, was to be the last of his copiously illustrated 'de luxe' books produced by Batsford. In this work, based on lectures originally delivered to the University of Bristol, Richardson covered a wide range of subjects extending from the armed services, religion, trade and industry to recreation, sport, drama, music, literature, painting and sculpture. In certain respects, this formed a kind of gloss to the impressive collection he had developed at Ampthill which covered all these areas with the same pioneering discernment and enthusiasm. His crusading zeal was undiminished and the book drew attention in particular to the decorative and building crafts at a time when the appreciation of the Georgian achievement was reaching an all-time low. In 1932 he was to play a leading role in the opposition to the Crown Commissioners' stated intention of demolishing Nash's Carlton House Terrace and again, in 1937, over the wanton destruction of the Adam Brothers' Adelphi, which brought about the formation of the Georgian Group with his active support.

figure 21
Giacomo Quarenghi (1744–1817), English Palace and Park, Peterhof (drawing from Richardson's collection)

figure 22
The White Hart, Scole, Norfolk, from *The Old Inns of England*, 1934

In the years following the Second World War, Richardson's committed scholarship, deep understanding of the British tradition and much of his creative energy were devoted to an energetic programme of restoration where he was able to draw on an almost unrivalled familiarity with the practical application of classicism. Prominent among these commissions were Wren's St James, Piccadilly; Hawksmoor's St Alfege, Greenwich; Gibbs's Senate House, Cambridge; John Wood the Elder's Assembly Rooms, Bath; Mylne's Trinity House, and Merchant Taylors Hall. After retiring from the Chair at the Bartlett in 1946, the following year he became Professor of Architecture at the Royal Academy (the first since 1911) and he continued in that position until 1960 with an opportunity to expound views which were no longer to be found in other schools. Within that period he became President of the Academy (1954–56), during which he consciously promoted the classic principles of his revered predecessors, Chambers, Soane and Cockerell, as well as actively promoting an ambitious pioneering exhibition at Burlington House which reassessed the applied and decorative as well as the fine arts of his revered period, English taste in the Eighteenth Century.[32]

figure 23
Robert Adam (1728–92), Edinburgh University 1785, drawing by Richardson from *An Introduction to Georgian Architecture*, 1949

In 1951 he had edited and contributed to a collection of essays on Henry Holland's finest surviving house and furnished interiors at Southill, Bedfordshire, where he had long enjoyed a close relationship with the Whitbread family as friend and adviser.[33] Perhaps nowhere else in Britain does one come closer to Richardson's ideal of classicism as the basis of good practical and rational design than in the formal reticence and application of fine detail throughout this house. Its custom-built fittings and furniture similarly represent a unique fusion of late 18th-century French and English classicism within a building and a series of interior spaces which are perennially fresh and enlivening. Two years earlier, he produced a brief volume which, despite its modest scale, may be regarded as Richardson's testament of design. In *An Introduction to Georgian Architecture*, illustrated by a wealth of his vivid sketches, he attempted to identify these elusive qualities at Southill. In his words: 'the secret of Holland's remarkable and exquisite taste rests in his own power of selecting proven motifs. There is shown that zest for inquiry and common sense which lies at the root of all the finest classic architecture. Holland was a realist in absolute fidelity to the facts and qualities of antique masterpieces. This love of detail for its own sake – of minor effects subtly ordered, precisely finished, richly simple and irresistible – points its own moral. The most exacting realism is adorned and enriched by all the resources of artistic skill; at the same time there is a complete suppression of meretricious pomposity.'[34]

Some ten years later, the completed design for Bracken House – one of his last major buildings – was to demonstrate all the formal resources and artistic skills which came from a lifetime of studying, expounding and practising those classical principles. The sequence of facades not only combined those qualities of formal coherence and classic restraint in composition advocated in *Monumental Classic Architecture*, within a particularly sensitive urban space close to Wren's St Paul's, but displayed a mastery of detail which stemmed from years of close study of classical ornament and appropriate material finish. As he had expressed it in his *Introduction to Georgian Architecture*, 'if we would capture the spirit of Georgian architecture, how should we set about the task? Not by the blind imitation of form, not by the mere revival of the phases of the style; for continuity does not flourish in this way. On the contrary we should try to understand its realism, its refined austerity, its clarity and its logic. All these attributes form part of the general make-up; but welding them all, there is another force which animates and determines the rest. This is the classic spirit which for more than two centuries has shone like a beacon to guide the architects of England. It was the unfailing principle and the definite goal of art.'[35]

figure 24
Albert Richardson *c.*1903

Some Memories

W.A.DOWNE, F.I.A.A.

When I was introduced by Professor Adshead to Richardson & Gill early in the year 1910 they rented two small rooms and a still smaller room which one could call a box room at 46 Great Russell Street, opposite the main front of the British Museum.[1] They had at that time only just left their employment as assistants to Frank T. Verity, a well-established architect who had been responsible for a large number of buildings in the West End. He was appropriately referred to by Richardson as 'The Beard'. The rooms on the floor above were occupied by Stanley Adshead who had been professor of Architecture at Liverpool University before the time of another architect of some renown – Professor Reilly.[2] Adshead was a very much older man than Richardson and had advised Richardson on matters of architecture and referred to him as one of the coming great men in the profession. He was polite but only in general on nodding terms with Gill who incidentally gave the impression that he thought Adshead rather an old dodderer. Adshead was rather of the dreamy and slow-moving type and was referred to quite respectfully by Richardson as 'The Old Adder'.

Upon my entering into their office at the inclusive salary of 2/6d. per week they employed two architectural assistants who had also been in Verity's office. They were T. Llewelyn Daniel and J.D. Benson Greenhall who departed to set up practice separately before the First War.

When I became the general factotum, varying the usual office boy duties with intervals spent in tracing, they had not been too successful in obtaining architectural commissions. They were carrying out alterations to Gill's parents' home in Dawlish in Devon, the enlargement of a house for a retired army officer at Hutley in Sussex and the rebuilding of No.19 Berkeley Street. These three jobs were brought into the office by Gill. Richardson was engaged on his first book, *London Houses* and I imagine as a matter of tact associated Gill with him as joint author. By the way, Gill was interested in photography as a hobby and was responsible for some of the photographs.

It was not long however before two useful commissions presented themselves. The first afforded a sound base for their future activities. This was their appointment as Architects to the Prince of Wales's estate in Devon and Cornwall. Adshead, with his interest in Richardson's progress, was responsible for this. Adshead with a partner, S.C. Ramsey, was architect to the Prince of Wales's large London estate at Kennington. The other commission was for the building of a new theatre at Manchester. In this case they were associated with an architect named Farquharson. Actually Gill knew the latter better than Richardson but Farquharson was really interested in dependence on a designer of Richardson's calibre.

Within a year, Gill obtained commissions that allowed them to take a much brighter outlook towards future security. These commissions were the design and erection of a large block of shops and offices in Finsbury Pavement and a large building which when completed was called Moorgate Hall. The firm who gave Richardson the opportunity of carrying out this work were solicitors in Old Broad Street who provided the money as a property investment company. A junior partner of this family firm was a cousin of Gill's. The senior partner was a very formidable and crusty person and I well knew it for I came in for considerable verbal punishment from him as the telephone was located in the 'Box Room' in which I dwelt. He was a person who in the middle of instructions or messages suddenly bawled, 'Have you got it?', 'Are you listening?' This method of transmitting his personal wrath to a youngster of my age was inclined to put me out of my stride with the result that a sometimes incomplete message to Gill provided Gill with an easy opportunity of lashing me. Gill himself was shaken now and again by the shattering drive of this old solicitor, but Richardson was literally scared by him and if he thought that I had answered the phone to him he violently signalled that he was out. The fact is that this business tycoon had absolutely no time for Richardson as he could not follow matters of design and had no appreciation for art at all. However, the work – and more was to follow from these solicitors – was far too valuable to allow them to counter the occasional bullying but Gill bore the brunt of his onslaught. It was Gill who brought in some quite big and useful work in the nature of alterations to large city buildings by his acquaintance with a firm of Estate Agents in the City of London.

Having completed *London Houses* and after it was published by Batsfords, Richardson got well into his stride with *Monumental Classic Architecture in Great Britain and Ireland.* Old Batsford proved to be almost a replica of the Broad Street solicitor and had Richardson at times hopping about as if he were treading on hot coals. What with Richardson's activities as a lecturer at that time with the London Polytechnic, his research work in connection with his writings, in the Library of the RIBA, and the persistent demands by his publisher for Richardson's presence, there were several near ruptures in the partnership.

With work coming in at a good pace and office accommodation being rather cramped they moved to more spacious offices at 41 Russell Square. They still had three rooms but they were all much larger than those in Great Russell Street and the work proceeded on a reasonably even keel.

In those days the partners were more or less entirely dependent in their different ways on each other. Gill had no ability at all on matters of design although at times he seemed to think he did and Richardson calmly suggested to him 'you do that one – you do this one, Charles', but this was only tact and on some 'backyard work'. Constructionally and contractually Gill to my mind was as near perfect as anyone in the profession could be. Richardson had some knowledge of construction but did not take it at all seriously. His contractual ability was negligible. He was of course a master in the use of a pencil and a genius in the creative art of building. Neither would have climbed to the heights they did if in the early days they were on their own.

Gill as a man was very sharp tempered and could use a few choice words at times with devastating effect. He was a tall man, upright in bearing with a brushed-up moustache and many people viewed him as a service man in mufti. He was a Devonshire parson's son. He was brusque with his draughtsmen but they were of an age of some stability and accepted Gill in his various moods.

As far as I was concerned for a year or so he had no patience with me at all. Whilst I was coping with all the normal office jobs (we did not have a typewriter in those early days so I took down his dictation in longhand and wrote the letters with copying ink) I was going ahead with my architectural studies with the occasional drawing in the office and evening work at the Polytechnic, helped very much with tuition from Richardson when he had the opportunity. Gill I think for a long while rather resented the fact that I was obtaining 'free education' when the profession in those exclusive days was partly based on the student taking articles. Actually as time went on the firm consistently found room in the office for students under the terms of 'Articling'. My youthful reply to persistent nagging was periodically to give notice. Whilst to all intents by his manner these intended counter-attacks seemed acceptable to Gill, some fatherly feeling from Richardson resulted in a withdrawal of this threat to depart.

I am sure the partnership would not have lasted long if Richardson had not been a genius for producing such great feats in design. Gill was prepared to shoulder the majority of the worry of office administration and building site supervision when the job started as well as the responsibility for the preparation of plans, etc. and to accept the fact that Richardson's mind was shared by lecturing and writing with the production of a masterpiece when it was required. After all, Gill shared the great credit that Richardson's work deserved and it was interesting to notice when, after many promises from Richardson to get the design started, with a superhuman effort at the last minute Richardson presented his artistic contribution and Gill, all strain removed, preened himself and gazed with pride as if he was solely responsible for the design. There is no doubt that Gill should be given the greatest credit for the load he carried in a time when builders were becoming more independent and the administrators of building bylaws were putting more and more difficulties in the way of architects.

Referring to the work Richardson really obtained from the Duchy of Cornwall, Gill was in his early days not so appreciative as he should have been although I did notice that as time went on he showed more interest. The reason, I felt, was that the building operations were mainly for alterations and extensions to the farmhouses, Duchy Offices, etc. and called for a knowledge of traditional local details. Whilst Richardson enjoyed this work he did not lose sight of the fact that although it was small it needed to be done properly and he looked forward to the monumental opportunities for design as well. Richardson made occasional visits to Devon and Cornwall and was very much at home and popular with the local craftsmen, so Gill left it to him to make his visits. At heart Gill had no time for the typical country and provincial town builder who was not backward in adding to his building trade designation such words as 'wheelwright & undertaker'.

I have never seen Richardson lose his temper and he was the essence of kindness. Whilst he was proud of his achievements he gave his assistants from the lowest upwards the impression that there was nobody in particular in charge. All was one continuously jolly party. In practice this attitude is not really successful but everybody treated him with the utmost respect. He had no idea of the importance of time and before giving his lectures at the Polytechnic or later at London University he would hold up the office work for a considerable time by giving his assistants a talk inclusive of a display of lantern slides – and talk as if he was giving a real lecture – quite oblivious of the stoppage of office work. These occasions were of course marked by the fact that Gill was out. I well remember one afternoon the gathering of all assistants in a semi-circle when, holding one of his lantern slides up to the light with his right hand, the door opened and Gill entered. The slide was dropped into his left hand and with his right hand still in position he pointed to the strings and cornices of the British Museum seen from the window and proceeded to give instructions upon details of mouldings that had reference to full size work several assistants were working on at their drawing boards.

I never remember him taking a holiday in the early days. He went down to Cornwall and Devon occasionally to settle some detail with the builders there, armed with one of his renowned sketch books. These books, before I left their employment some two years after the First War, filled two large drawers in a bureau and it was amazing how he never seemed to have any difficulty in putting his hand very quickly on the book that contained a certain sketch that he wished to show me.

One part of my duties was the holding of money for use as petty cash. Gill used to let me have a sovereign which should have gone a long way and when I had expended this on the usual small stuff such as stamps, envelopes, fares etc. I asked for more. Richardson was an inveterate borrower with his requests for taxi fares. He went to almost everywhere in an area which included the RIBA and Batsfords by taxi and he never seemed to have the money in his pocket to cover this at times unnecessary expenditure. This was a matter that naturally caused me to come into some collision with Gill. Whilst I was happy to support Richardson, it was pretty obvious that taxi fares quickly disposed of the cash. Gill had of course access to my petty cash book and demanded that I should refuse to give Richardson money for taxis when he asked for it. At times when I presented him with this ultimatum he pretended to see some reason but often beat me by pointing out on arriving at the office out of breath that there was a taxi at the door. When I said I had almost run out of petty cash he now and again said, 'You have got some money in your pocket, let me have what you can and ask Gill for some more.' These seemingly unscrupulous methods did not help my relationship with Gill but as I grew older and my timidity was gradually being shaken off I took a more determined stand and advised Gill that it was up to him to keep Richardson in check.

Richardson did not seem to have any people who could be called friends in a general way. His whole time was spent with his art but he did bring under his wing Hanslip Fletcher who was an etcher of some distinction. For years his works appeared regularly in *The Times* but Richardson's real appreciation for him I think was that he was a master at architectural perspective and detail.[3]

Just after the war Richardson somehow or other managed to persuade Gill to let Fletcher put a table and chair in the smaller room. He only used the room occasionally and spent a lot of time in the basement where he printed his etchings. Gill, who was always interested in wood and had a great knowledge of timber in general, suddenly took to making violins and he became quite an expert and sold these instruments at very good prices. He spent quite a lot of time in the office picking up and examining his particular selection as it was seasoning and then took further time in whittling it down to the required size and shape. His efforts in this respect thoroughly pleased Richardson who I remember one day coming in and, on opening the front room door, seeing Gill busily engaged with his hobby. He shut the door and turning round to me pointed with a giggle to the room and said, 'That will keep him quiet!'

I might quote the words used by Richardson to me when I was leaving their employ: 'There is one thing my boy, you will never fail to get work as an architect when you mention that you have been with us.' How correct this was.

A Discriminating Taste

SIMON HOUFE

figure 25
Silver-Gilt cup presented to Gonville & Caius College, Cambridge, by General Sir Bruce Meade Hamilton, GCB, KCVO, and Officers of the General Staff, First Army, Central Force, in Memory of 1915

In 1914, an American architect, a member of the renowned McKim, Mead and White Partnership, visited A.E. Richardson's grand town house offices at No 41 Russell Square, in the heart of Bloomsbury.

'It was one of those late Georgian, capacious and generously proportioned houses, evidently the home of consequential persons in its day. We were ushered into a great front salon with the usual informality of an architect's sanctum, and our new acquaintance rose from his seat at a long table and greeted us with some enthusiasm.... He launched forth into his particular admirations, his architectural treasury, and began to bring forth books and great folios. We had neither of us heard of Schinkel, and his dismay at our having missed the author of the Brandenburg Gate in Berlin, which has since become so much a part of the news, was at once corrected by the exhibition of the monumental edition of his works.'[1]

Such a description gives some indication of just how important Richardson considered his immediate surroundings. The appearance of a 'salon' with its 'long table' and an admirable 'architectural treasury' close to hand were to be repeated in other houses and to impress other visitors in the following fifty years.

Richardson's first tentative steps in forming a 'glossary' of taste were to be found in his own room in the parental house just off the Heath at Hampstead. A well-designed oil lamp, a single oak table and prints on the wall were the adjuncts of a budding architectural apprentice. It was certainly in contrast to his parents' anti-macassars and figurines! He was at this time studying with the minor architect Victor Page in the Grays Inn Road.

The move to Evelyn Hellicar's office at Sergeant's Inn in 1898 was a world away from the Gray's Inn Road. He was suddenly in the orbit of serious architects, designers with a philosophy of style and clients of taste and wealth. It was the end of the reign of 'Queen Anne'; Hellicar being a Kent architect was inclined to have patrons that had lingered in that golden age longer than most. Substantial villas and country houses flowed from his drawing-board with trim brickwork, white panelled halls and bolection mould chimney pieces. Richardson recalled it all with affection in his diary fifty years later when he visited one of them, Bingham's Melcombe, 1897–98.

'I was carried back to the earliest days of my career at No 10 Sergeant's Inn where I learnt my architecture as a youth. I thought of Evelyn Hellicar arriving each morning at 10 o'clock from Bromley, Kent, how well I remember his familiar footstep on the staircase, he was a mild tempered gentleman, a fine artist and watercolourist. I saw his work from the standpoint of today, almost fifty-seven years had elapsed and it stood the test very well. I noticed the profile of the mouldings re-echoing Jackson's teaching. The grates from Longden's. The C & I plain waterheads from Dent & Hellyer. The locks from Elsleys and what struck a very forcible note the wallpaper by William Morris.'[2]

Surprisingly it is this link with Morris and the Arts and Crafts Movement, nurtured in the Hellicar practice, that was the most abiding feature of Richardson's earliest homes. The 'Queen Anne' fascination with polished surfaces and blue and white china was certainly digested, but more importantly the all embracing credo of good craftsmanship and fitness for purpose was imbibed. In March 1903, Richardson made the change from a domestic to a more ecclesiastical architectural office, that of Leonard Stokes of Great Smith Street, well known for college and institutional buildings. It was to be a short sojourn with this querulous man, barely ten months. The increase in salary gave the courage to propose marriage! In June 1903, Richardson crossed over to Ireland to marry the love of his life Elizabeth Byers at Newry in County Down. Their first home together was the touchstone of his belief in the Arts and Crafts tradition. Some rooms were taken just off Heath Street, Hampstead (he was always beguiled by North London) and at once filled with Richardson's carefully acquired possessions. They were at once 'Queen Anne' and Arts and Crafts, the ubiquitous Dutch dresser decorated with pottery, the well used Windsor chairs, a good old escritoire in the background and a paper frieze in the manner of Burne-Jones. In addition to this there was a large photograph of York Minster (always a favourite) a photogravure of a Georgian scene and two framed panels of Richardson's own minute watercolours. These were in reality the decorated envelopes sent to Elizabeth during their courtship, little romantic gems of eighteenth-century London, her native Ireland or the railway, the stamp and address carefully incorporated into the design![3]

figure 26
Frank T. Verity

This was the main living room of the young couple and they at once got a photographer friend in to photograph it from every angle, grainy sepias complete with an open copy of the *Burlington Magazine* (founded that year) on the table.

There is no hint of any architect-designed furniture except for the clock on the mantelpiece. This was surely Richardson's own invention, a simple tapered wooden frame with a slight hint of *art nouveau* or even Voysey about it! He had already encountered C.F.A. Voysey in the offices of his new employer Leonard Stokes at Great Smith Street.

In November 1903, Richardson made the transition from sombre Westminster to the more frivolous West End, when he became improver to Frank Verity, the theatre architect in Sackville Street. This move presaged a change of style as well as a change of location, but at first the only difference was an increase in salary and a more commodious home. Within the year, the Richardsons had moved into 15 Denning Road, Hampstead, a Victorian terraced house which he began to alter. Elizabeth Richardson was expecting a baby and Richardson's

figure 27
Interior of Richardson's first married home, No.15 Denning Road, Hampstead, 1903

efforts were directed towards creating an artistic home for his wife and daughter and their growing circle.

He was still at heart the Arts & Crafts designer, nurtured by the Hellicar office and fired by the good ecclesiastical workmanship that he had seen on Stokes' drawing-boards. He set about to design all his own furniture for Denning Road, the beds, the wash-stands, oak settles and simple chests. He was immensely proud of getting the local carpenter to run up a settle for £2 from his own design (and continued to advocate this when Master of the Art Workers Guild forty years later). Nor did he forget that symbol of Edwardian respectability the piano. One can follow the genesis of this substantial instrument through several sketch-books; first a cabinet with doors swinging open to reveal the keyboard, then a sideboard with prominent candlestands. Finally it became a black grained up-right with deep mouldings and strange attenuated shafts reaching to the floor from the end of the keyboard. Its angularity has slight affinities with Mackin-tosh or some of the Glasgow artists.[4] The same sketch-book has a pencil draw-ing of Raymond Unwin's Hampstead office, showing the sort of company he kept.

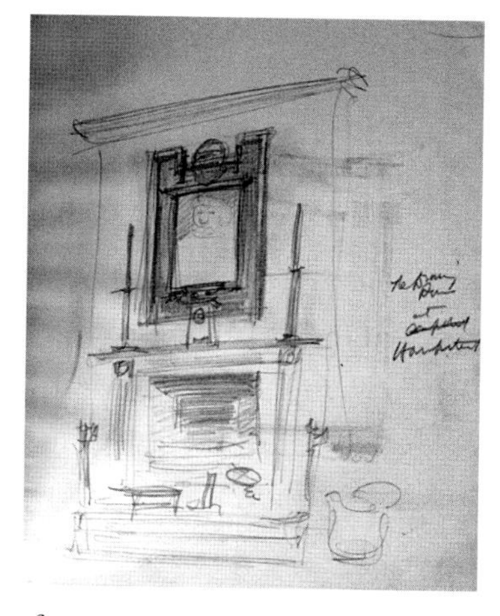

figure 28
Overmantel in Denning Road

The great problem in this compact Hampstead house was to create a setting from unpromising material. The front room had an ungainly marble fireplace on over-sized brackets and this had to be lost. He installed good photogravures in oak frames designed by himself and, over the mantelpiece, a Frans Hals repro-duction in an extraordinary oak frame with moulded sides and horns above it, giving it height and emphasis.[5]

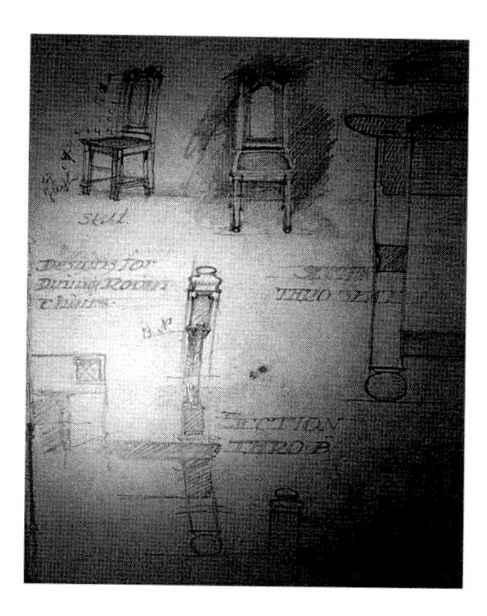

figure 29
Design for dining room chairs, from a sketchbook *c.*1903

At the same time he kept a visual check-list of the furniture that he had seen, in museums, in a corner of Birkbeck College, in dealers' shops, meticulous pen-cil drawings with notes attached or perhaps a price. One such page is inscribed 'Jottings from Chancellor's Old Furniture, March 9th 1903.'[6] It is still the glean-ings of a devotee of Wrenish and Queen Anne-ish things with a high proportion of oak coffers and gate-leg tables. Significantly another page has 'Dining Room furniture based on old examples'.

At the back of the house, a small garden was created with a sunken area of flags in the middle surrounding a sundial of his own devising. This formality was circled by a row of small evergreen trees giving a rather Italian effect. At heart, he was very metropolitan and flowers did not move him at all!

The free use of Chancellor's book and the gradual interest in Georgian furni-ture, denoted another contact, Herbert Batsford of High Holborn. He had been wandering into that great emporium since the late 'nineties and Batsford had befriended him. By 1908 he was talking to Batsford about a book which was eventually to appear as *London Houses*, a logical step towards his involvement with the domestic interior.

The six years in which he was right-hand man to Frank Verity were crucial in broadening Richardson's horizons and altering his outlook. Thomas Bennett, who worked for Richardson in 1910, recalled Verity's teasing Richardson over his Arts & Crafts appearance, cycling knickerbockers, Norfolk jackets and flan-nel shirts! Verity's dandified figure with his finely trimmed beard, cream waist-coat and watch chain was a far cry from the conventional Hellicar or the ascetic Stokes. Richardson fell for the swagger and the panache of Verity's No 7 Sackville Street where smart clients arrived by motor, lived in mansion flats designed by the master and were at home at theatres and in café society. More importantly it was what Verity admired that fired Richardson with enthusiasm; a whole world of Parisian architecture and culture was opened up for him as he, and the other young assistant C.L. Gill, were escorted to the boat train and taken on tours of Paris.

The sketch-books were now crammed with details of Louis Quinze and Louis Seize architecture, the works of Blondel, Jacques-Ange Gabriel and Boffrand.

Verity's father had come to prominence under the Second Empire, so there was much enthusiasm for the street architecture of Napoleon III, lamp standards, grilles and iron gates. Equally exciting were the great works of the previous generation, Hittorf's Gare du Nord, the Palais de Justice by Duc, and the works of Duban and Labrouste.

The love of the dix-huitiéme was all the rage in London, where Arthur Davis of the Parisian firm of Méwes & Davis was constructing the Royal Automobile Club in Pall Mall and where Frank Verity's theatre interiors had Gallic resonances. Edith Wharton's *The Decoration of Houses* had focussed the eyes of the rich on this period and a French revival ran concurrently with the Adam and Chippendale revival of the Edwardians. However great the enthusiasm, it was definitely not an area in which an impecunious young architect could dabble, so Richardson continued to espouse the Arts and Crafts in his home life and to buy some sturdy oak pieces for his rooms. In fact, around 1910 he was eschewing the antique trade altogether. In a small essay for a forgotten periodical *The Folio* he sets down his thoughts at Christmastime in the 'Furniture Craze'.

'If we must collect old furniture instead of having our tables and chairs made for us, as we are measured for our clothes, surely it would be wiser to choose our examples from a period, the conditions of which, very nearly approximate to those which prevail today. Away with gim-crack Elizabethan Houses and furniture – very fine pieces of theatricism, no doubt, and very suitable for a museum, but to live with them, emphatically no. It is not playing the game, we should need to don doublets and hose and put up with frightful inconveniences, and if we act our part faithfully, walk to town every day. The same treatment should be meted out to all the fantasies of the Georgian era. Aldermanic chairs, cumbersome tables, coarse shapes, away with them, bundle them into a museum, hold them up as objects of past comfort. Interesting as relics, some pieces are really beautiful, but priceless only as far as the public demand for them is concerned.

'All revivals of the Antique are deplorable. Reproductions arrest the development of modern design whether in Furniture or Architecture. L'Art Nouveau has burnt itself out; its exponents attempted too much without paying due respect to the works of the past. All the best articles of furniture design are the result of easy transposition from similar objects of like design, the transposition embodying the original idea with such refining influences as suggested themselves to the craftsman. The Arts of Architecture and furniture design have fallen very low in England, when old-time shapes are reproduced on every side without any regard to modern needs.'[7]

In another contribution of the same date, Richardson highlights the quandary of the contemporary architect.

'We have witnessed during the past quarter of a century a determined effort on the part of designers to resuscitate the charming homeliness of character associated with the great periods of building tradition. Yet, widespread as the movement is, its success can only be regarded as partial. Two factors have contributed to focalize public attention on this important branch of architecture, the first being the abnormal spread of architectural literature and photographic illustration, the second the universality of the collecting habit. Although a certain standard of taste has resulted, a strange medley of dissimilar styles now, nevertheless, do duty as backgrounds to the changed conditions of modern life.'[8]

His increasing passion for French classical architecture under the tutelage of Frank Verity, was enriched by his meeting with R. Phené Spiers, an architect and draughtsman and one of the few men in the profession trained in the Atelier Questel-Pascal.[9] These interests were leading him into an investigation of British buildings of a parallel date. This was to culminate in his great work, *Monumental Classic Architecture in Great Britain and Ireland*, published in 1914. His, by now frequent, articles in the *Architectural Review* and the *Architect's Journal* were appealing to a younger generation who wanted a classical revival which would assimilate a national style. In July 1911, he wrote an article on 'The Style Neo-Grec' which, as well as showing important works by Schinkel and Duc, related these to the monumental architecture being produced in Britain in the period 1790 to 1830.[10] This was a quite new departure in the profession, which had tended to look with contempt on anything post 1750.

Four months later he launched into two further articles on 'The Empire Style in England', November and December 1911, which were indeed breaking new ground. Here for the first time was a comprehensive survey of interior decoration in the early years of the nineteenth century. Characteristically, he wrote on the top page of his copy of this piece 'This article started the fashion for Regency.' In about five pages, he attempted to raise the profile of the English Empire style as it had not been trumpeted for eighty years and particularly to draw attention to Thomas Hope. 'Following the fashion of the day, he [Hope] collected a large number of valuable antique marbles, which were housed in his London house in Duchess Street, Cavendish Square, and afterwards at the classic villa he built as a country seat at Deepdene, near Dorking. Hope's taste for furniture was remarkable, as may be seen by reference to his important work on the subject. He attempted to raise furniture design from the rank of a cringing second-rate art practised by tradesmen to the level of a living and first-rate art closely allied to architecture.'[11] Richardson praised the purity of the style which was such an excellent exemplar for modern architects. 'The special point of interest with regard to the English interior decoration of the period is in the absolute non-inclusion of such architectural features as stereotyped columns and entablatures as decorative adjuncts to a room. The interest is concentrated entirely on the design of the furniture and the other appointments, the walls being simply used as backgrounds to the movable furniture, carpets and curtains.' These comments were accompanied by superb illustrations of Carlton House and Buckingham Palace from Pyne's *Royal Residencies*, 1818.

figure 30
Thomas Hope (1769–1831), 'Flaxman's Aurora visiting Cephalus on Mount Ida', at Duchess Street, from *Household Furniture and Decoration*, 1807 (illustrated in Richardson's article 'The Empire Style in England', 1911)

In the second article, he concentrated on furniture and used many of the fine line engravings from Hope's magnum opus *Household Furniture and Interior Decoration*, 1807. 'While the influence of Classic research lasted, furniture design was stimulated to an unprecedented degree; when this influence waned, partly owing to the decline of interest in the Antique, and the consequent lack of an appreciative audience, the character of movables and other architectural accessories suffered.' In defining the style, Richardson wrote: 'For convenience the style of the Regency is named 'Empire'; in reality the furniture of the period epitomises the tendencies which formed the style. The desire expressed on every side was for decorative art approaching in beauty, as well as in interest and utility, the Art of Ancient Greece.'[12] It was in this way that he was credited with coining the phrase 'Regency' in England as an article as opposed to a political term.[13]

In conclusion, he underlined that this golden age should be marked out as a yardstick of taste. 'A mere donning of the antique cloak will not suffice to advance modern art. To help artists in the great neo-Classic movement which is daily becoming more apparent it will be necessary to enlist the sympathy of the whole educational body.'

In 1908, Richardson had left Verity's office in order to set up in practice with C.L. Gill, although both young men retained links with him for a few years. Their modest success (mostly from Gill's wealthy cousins) enabled Richardson to branch out in a new direction in 1909, the purchase of a genuine house of the Regency period. Having been raised in Hampstead and enjoyed long walks with his father deep into the Home Counties, he was attracted to Hertfordshire. His choice fell on Cavendish House, St Albans, a flint-faced villa of the 1790s with untouched interiors and within easy walking distance of the railway.

Cavendish House fulfilled his desire to collect and experiment with the

Regency interior. Over the next five years he acquired design books and original drawings of the period from Batsford's secondhand department and furniture from the curio shops of the cathedral city. By 1914 the rooms had been decorated with simple refinement, striped wall-paper (an innovation in 1914), a floral carpet and restrained coverings to the furniture in claret colours. The pieces themselves were mostly Empire, a scroll end settee, ormolu clock, Adam overmantel mirror and Coalbrookdale ornaments. It was a first attempt to clarify and categorise a forgotten epoch. The rooms were photographed by the St Albans studio of Mr Cherry and published to aid his campaign for a new dynamic of classical architecture.

Writing at this time in *The Estate Magazine* he said, 'We have everything to gain from the careful study of bygone styles, providing we do not become slaves

figure 31
Interior at Cavendish House, St Alban's, 1909

to their mannerisms. The artistic culture of the past is by no means a lost art; it is true that the local colour and sympathy of its own age have passed from it. Time has effaced all that at one period appeared commonplace; but its truths, viewed from a distance, when they can be judged more accurately, appeal to us as approaching the ideal.'[14]

It is not surprising that one of his first commissions in his new county should be for the antique dealer William C. Angell at Radlett, Hertfordshire. Angell had known Richardson from a child and gave him the opportunity to create a small shop and dwelling in the Regency idiom facing on to Watling Street. Great care was taken in the fenestration and glazing and the two storeys were crowned with a dormer in a gambrel roof. The building was carried out from the foundations between 1909 and 1910, the architect calling in on his way home from London in the evening. He was also a good client of Angell, purchasing from him at about this time all the furniture (Regency of course) for the Board Room of the *Architect's Journal* at 27–29 Tothill Street, Westminster.[15]

Richardson regarded the years 1914 to 1918 as a void in his career, when old friendships were tragically ended and a blossoming practice was curtailed. Before joining up in 1916, he was able to write a penetrating article on the Arts and Crafts Exhibition at the Royal Academy in which he was surprisingly generous to scorned contemporaries. While castigating the work of Gimson he considered 'Mr and Mrs Charles Mackintosh are to the front.'[16] For three years he was in the Royal Flying Corps at Southampton, in charge of salvaging aeroplanes damaged on the Western Front. With characteristic ingenuity, he started a cottage industry in the RFC workshops, making classical ornaments for the mantelpiece out of rejected aircraft parts! These were sold with some success in the Southampton area! Returning to civilian life in December 1918, he was short-listed for the vacant Bartlett Chair of Architecture at University College, London. This was largely on the strength of his book *Monumental Classic Architecture* and his Carpenters Company lectures of 1913. The Bartlett Professor was expected to live within forty miles of the College. Richardson was tired of St Albans, which he considered was being spoiled by villas,[17] and he began to search for a home further away from London's sprawl.

He remembered early holidays in Bedfordshire[18] and in particular a training march in 1915 which had taken him through the small town of Ampthill, where he had admired a Georgian town house then unoccupied. Returning to Ampthill by train, he found the house to let, and after some delays succeeded in buying it in June 1919. Ampthill was slightly over the prescribed mileage limit for the Bartlett, but he conveniently forgot about that! Avenue House dated from the end of the eighteenth century and because it had been occupied by only one family was little changed. There was no electricity, scarcely any modern conveniences and every cornice, fireplace and door handle was in place. For the next forty-six years, he made his house a measuring scale of everything he did, its details endlessly inspired new works, its collections acted as a glossary and its library was consulted by scholars. It was also a focus for many young architects and writers in the 1920s and 1930s, the Bartlett students were transported down to Bedfordshire by charabanc and danced on the lawns and some of the early founders of the Georgian Group were invited for weekends.

Among the earlier visitors were Brendan Bracken, then running *English Life*, Margaret Jourdain, R.W. Symonds, the furniture historian, the artists Sylvia Pankhurst and Nan West and the Italian lecturer in English at Liverpool. Among the older generation of architects, J. Alfred Gotch, and among the younger, Arthur Davis, Charles Holden, Charles Reilly with his son Paul, Alfred Bossom, Claude Phillimore, Robert Lutyens and Lord Gerald Wellesley. From America came the architectural historian H. Donaldson Eberlein, who stayed for long periods, Fiske Kimball, expert on the eighteenth century, and Thomas Waterman, the first architect of Colonial Williamsburg. A little later came John and Penelope Betjeman, Christopher and Elizabeth Hussey and Jim Lees-Milne.

A Regency town house created the right background for his teaching and writing. Avenue House became the catalyst for half a dozen books, notably the acclaimed *Georgian England*, 1931. The rooms and the objects contained in them were used in his books and articles and the house featured in a number of publications between the Wars, particularly in *Homes and Gardens*, *Country Life* and various magazines associated with Basil Ionides. His collecting had settled down to a steady acquisition of the golden age 1790 to 1810 with occasional flutters into early Georgian. He had always bought exclusively from dealers, never the auctions or country house sales. A busy life probably precluded this, although he obtained many of the catalogues and must have perused them. He did not attend the Hope sale in 1917 (although stationed nearby) but may have attended that at Cassiobury in 1922. His buying was mostly done from those dealers within walking distance of his Bloomsbury office or from country dealers at weekends.

His friendship with Margaret Jourdain must have begun about 1920. On visits to Avenue House she was shown neighbouring collections, such as that at Crawley Park, which she later published. This connection must have led to Richardson's close relationship with the firm of Lenygon & Morant, for whom Jourdain worked. They in turn were associated with White Allom, the firm of the highly successful decorator Sir Charles Allom who worked for the Royal Family and rich Americans. The two younger members of this establishment, Frank

Surgey and Murray Adams Acton, were certainly friends and sold Richardson small antiques. These were the halcyon days of 'the period room' – huge panelled chambers were dismantled from demolished mansions and packed off to the United States, the trade was awash with bits and pieces conveniently reassembled by architects manqué! Richardson certainly never willingly acquiesced in this slightly bogus game, although he was forced by circumstances to do two reconstructions.[19]

An interesting reflection of his taste at this time was the small work he undertook for the Wembley Exhibition of 1924. It was decided that leading connoisseurs should be asked to decorate rooms in their favourite styles for the Palace of Arts. These included 'The 1750 Room', 'The 1815 Room', 'The 1852 Room', 'The 1888 Room', and 'The 1924 Rooms.' Richardson was naturally given the chance to design the '1815' one and borrowed a large collection of Thomas Hope pieces from a fellow enthusiast, the playwright, Edward Knoblock. In the centre was the carpet from Carlton House, which he had recently acquired from a Bond Street dealer and the painted Regency music-stand from Ampthill. The construction was carried out quite accurately by Jacksons & Sons, wall covering being specially woven by Mortimer's. R.W. Symonds writing in *Homes & Gardens* said: 'Notwithstanding the bias towards archaeology, such apartments have a stately effect without sacrifice of homely charm. Such a room as the one now seen at Wembley was familiar to the Regent at Buckingham Palace and Carlton House, and to Lord Byron in the Albany.'[20] There is no record of what he thought of the 1924 Rooms, designed by Gerald Wellesley and Trenwith Wills as a result of the *Country Life* competition; they are certainly light and airy with a Regency sparseness.

The rooms at Avenue House had already appeared in an article in *Country Life* on 2nd December 1922 written by Randall Phillips. Phillips noted that Richardson had recently removed the few Victorian accretions in the house and (with the assistance of Messrs Robersons) had decorated the rooms practically without pictures. He also adds, 'The saloon is the chief feature of Avenue House, but in all the other rooms is seen the good taste of the present owner, both in the matter of furniture and in the appropriate use of it. Professor Richardson, indeed, is not only happy in his possession, but also he knows how to respect the heritage of the past and at the same time to make it serve the needs of today.'[21] John Cornforth has pointed out that the very austerity of the saloon in 1922 has something almost proto-Modern about it.[22]

opposite · figure 32
The Saloon at Avenue House, Ampthill, 1922

figure 33
Sitting Room at Avenue House, drawing by Richardson

Visitors were already struck by the thematic arrangements within the rooms. The Professor of English Literature at Rome, who must have come in about 1922, recalled this in *The House of Life* '...the ... association of historical events ... led Professor Sir Albert Richardson, the architect, at his house at Ampthill in Bedfordshire, to hang a portrait of Nelson, in an oblong frame in the form of a piece of rope with loops at the upper and lower extremities, close to two models of the *Victory*, and near by, portraits of Napoleon and Josephine, a bronze sphinx and a chess-board, together with its chess-men, to symbolize the strategy of the war between the Emperor of the French and the great British Admiral.'[23] Oddly enough Napoleon and Nelson competed for attention in Richardson's affections and their images and those of their lady friends were everywhere!

By the mid-1920s, he had acquired some original Thomas Hope pieces and these were exhibited at the Loan Exhibition and Antiques Fair sponsored by the *Daily Telegraph* at Olympia in August 1928. The latter was organised by Margaret Jourdain and contained many exhibits from his friends as well as the ubiquitous panelled rooms from White Allom, Keebles and Gill & Reigate. He lent Hope's wall-lights from Duchess Street and some library furniture. At the same time as acquiring antiques, he was collecting architectural books, particularly the smaller pattern-books of the late eighteenth century and the Regency, neglected by connoisseurs. These were consulted regularly during his architectural projects, were an important resource for lectures and invaluable in compiling his own books. Furthermore, on the Burlington and Soane model, he was purchasing early architectural drawings for use in his office work.[24]

By the time that Christopher Hussey wrote the second *Country Life* article on the house in 1934, following the visit of Her Majesty Queen Mary, the decoration and the furnishing seemed almost complete, augmented by excellent English pictures. There is a shift from the rather angular pieces of the earlier years to the painted furniture of the 1790s and a softer and more feminine feel to the interiors. Hussey illustrated not only the saloon with its Sheraton desks and tables, but the more hum-drum parts of the house, such as the Old Kitchen which Richardson had filled with copper and brass of the period. Like all the early writers (and Richardson himself) he attributed the house to Holland, rather than his protégé John Wing. 'Professor Richardson may be said to have made it one of his life's works – in addition to the practice and, as chief instructor at University College, the inculcation of civil architecture – to reincarnate the most civilised of architects here in Ampthill.'[25]

From 1931 for about eight years, Richardson contributed short articles on collecting to his friend J. Robertson Scott's magazine the *Countryman*. They ranged from little essays on domestic silver to disquisitions on sofas and French prints, whatever interested him at that moment. He did not neglect country furniture and saltglaze pottery, warming pans and glass, inspired by his close friendship with Charles Wade of Snowshill Manor. Wade's reconstruction of Snowshill appealed to Richardson's arts and crafts side and he adopted a similar passion for models, trade bygones and old musical instruments. He wrote a very sympathetic article on Snowshill for *Country Life*.[26] He had a genius for collecting the unfashionable, the Regency when everyone collected early Georgian, baroque ivories when others would not look at them, pattern books when they were neglected and costume when it was discarded from country houses!

His connection with firms such as Lenygons continued in the 1930s and he used his dealer friends as quarries for his architectural work. An alteration for a city firm, the restoration of a country house or advice on a cathedral would often be completed by a judiciously selected lantern from Moss Harris or Pratt's or a fine piece of tapestry from S.W. Wolsey. His total reconstruction of St Mary's Church, Eaton Socon, was crowned by such purchases of fabric and he assisted in acquiring works for the Jockey Club at Newmarket and various livery com-

figure 34
Richardson's rooms at St Catherine's College, Cambridge, 1943, drawing by Hanslip Fletcher

pany halls. He was frequently asked his opinion by the 1st Lord Fairhaven who was building up his collection at Anglesey Abbey and assisted the 2nd Lord Stanmore in the same way.

The Second World War was as much a blow to his life's work as the First had been. The office closed and life at Ampthill curtailed. But an added bonus was that Richardson along with University College was evacuated to Cambridge and took up residence for five years at St Catherine's. He had always preferred clubable, donnish life to any other, and settled very easily into the gentle routine of early chapel, high table and civilised converse. T.R. Henn, later Master of St Catherine's, remembered him at this period. 'He loved nothing better than a bargain at some antique shop. He gave me a very lovely watercolour of his own which hangs in my rooms: and designed me a beautiful oak bookcase running along one side of my rooms. He seemed to know and be on terms with, all the craftsmen in Cambridge; and I remember he spent a lot of time with Rattee & Kett's foreman in getting the mouldings right.... He *lived* in the 18th century; patterns of quality, decorum, courtesy, proportion, grace of living, honesty, craftsmanship and he could always be "drawn" on this subject.'[27]

His rooms, slightly to the left of the porch at St Catherine's, inspired a seventeenth-century theme. He at once began collecting furniture in the gothick style, a magnificent gothick architect's table (eventually left to Strawberry Hill) a magisterial armchair, reputedly the property of Dean Swift and boxes and ivories that might have suited the Tradescants. In May 1943, his old friend Hanslip Fletcher came to stay at Cambridge and did a memorable pencil sketch of the room, the fireplace surrounded by ornaments, an elegant teapot waiting service on a trivet, a pencil barometer by the window and huge architectural tomes leaning crazily under the window. These important works had been acquired on various 'raids' on David's book-stall as and when the colleges had thrown them out! In this way he had added to his collection presentation works by Gibbs and from Evelyn's family. Facing the desk was a black framed Flemish 'Vanitas' to remind him of the futility of human wishes and elsewhere copper panels and Dutch interiors. In this setting he liked to sit, wreathed in cigar smoke, until such time that he put on fustian clothes and crept across the corridor to Dr Henn's haunted rooms and gave that poor don a considerable fright!

The return to London in 1945 marked a break with the past, the old partnership with Gill was terminated and the fine rooms at Russell Square vacated. He moved to 31 Old Burlington Street to occupy the top floor of Lenygon & Morant's celebrated Palladian house, where objects from Cambridge and Russell Square were united with others from Ampthill. The connection with Lenygon's continued, they helping to supply him with objects for special clients, he enjoying the atmosphere and making occasional purchases. The only confusion came when choice specimens bought by the Professor in Edinburgh or York ended up in Lenygon's stock!

The great rebuilding programme in London after the Blitz, in which he played so large a part, gave fresh impetus to his energy for furniture design. Although antiques were occasionally purchased for Trinity House, the Merchant Taylors Hall and bombed churches, the majority of the furnishing was architect designed. He had long patronised the Bedford firm of J.P. White & Sons of the Pyghtle Works, whose traditions went back into the Arts and Crafts movement. Perhaps Richardson's finest furniture was produced for Trinity House where so much had been destroyed, mahogany benches, side-tables, the Master's chair and dining-room furniture. It was always inspired by the classical past but fresh in concept and never slavishly copied, having his distinct imprint upon every part of it. This was also true of the author's table-desk designed for Winston Churchill at Chartwell or the cheval glass presented by Bedford Borough to Princess Elizabeth in 1947. Even closer to home was the furniture designed for the Sir Malcolm Stewart Community Hall at Stewartby, elegantly simple and fitting perfectly into his unique Scandinavian pavilion there.

In 1952, the move to 24 Queen Anne Street gave the excuse for more elaborate furnishing, this time in a 1760s house which he was to make a permanent London residence for many years. The first floor drawing-room became his office (shared with his able partner and son-in-law Eric Houfe). The walls were papered in deep green with gold stars, the carpet was a rich Savonerie and busts of Inigo Jones and Andrea Palladio were peeping between the columns of the window embrasure. In the centre of the window was a Regency harp and on one wall a vast pedimented Chippendale bookcase filled with early books and seal impressions. There were architectural models in this room, a bust of Madame Récamier by Chinard and drawings by Victor Louis and Clérisseau. The effect was of quiet and repose, although the bustling figure of Richardson, well on into his seventies, with rolls of drawings under his arm was scarcely tranquil.

figure 35
Side table and carpet designed by Richardson for Trinity House, Tower Hill, c.1953

At Ampthill, the rather stark classicism of the early *Country Life* photographs had given way to profusion. Each tour to the Continent or trip round the British Isles, resulted in yet more and more objects of association or inspiration, each with its breathlessly recounted story. James Lees-Milne visiting in August 1947 described it. 'It is chock-a-block with treasures. The Professor looks like a Rowlandson figure among so much Georgian elegance.'[28] He would have stoutly defended his eclecticism, for Avenue House was not intended to be an historical recreation so much as a bench mark of his own experience. His personality was imbued with the eighteenth-century concept of the amateur as well as with the nineteenth-century one of the aesthete, so on both counts it was a subjective display of taste. He was well aware of the deadening effects of historicism, so that his rooms were not so much a didactic as an experiential view of a period, he would have claimed their atmosphere as all important. Following on from Walpole and the de Goncourts, whom he admired, he aimed to distill the elements of style into a synthesis by suggestion and intuition rather than by direct imitation.

The walk through the rooms became an elaborate ritual. As Robert Wraight experienced on one of the last illustrated interviews in November 1961 – 'The house has been a continuous source of inspiration to Sir Albert in his work as an architect. "It gave me ideas for mouldings and other things for the Jockey Club at Newmarket and the Royal Pavilion at Ascot. And when Winston asked me to design a monument to bring America into the war, I got my idea from the drawing-room fireplace. I'll show you," he said and, lifting himself with remarkable agility from his deep wing-chair, he began what must surely be the most exhausting – and exhilarating – conducted tour of all the historic houses of England.'[29]

In these last two decades of his life, Richardson's approach was becoming less specialised and more catholic. The Arts and Crafts enthusiasm was still there in recreating an Elizabethan cottage on the estate, so was the Strawberry Hill antiquarianism that loved a relic.[30] But the greatest change was the growing realisation that the Victorian age had much to offer. From the 1930s when he had contributed articles on the Victorians to the *Countryman*, he had begun to acquire Victorian pictures and books and nineteenth-century Continental art. They were totally neglected at this time and only John Betjeman and Evelyn Waugh (whom he knew slightly) collected such things. The same strictures as to quality and historical significance pertained, but the period had moved forward. By a strange irony, the Professor had come full circle; the crowded table tops and the paintings of Queen Victoria represented once more for him something that he had seen in his youth.

[*Simon Houfe is at present working on Sir Albert Richardson's diaries with the intention of writing an architectural biography.*]

figure 36
Sir Albert Richardson at Avenue House, *c.*1960

figure 37
Bracken House, Cannon Street

Albert Richardson: a critical survey

ALAN POWERS

The last hundred years of architecture in Britain, including the time in which Sir Albert Richardson was active, can only begin to be understood when it is looked at in its entirety. Among its architects, perhaps only Sir Edwin Lutyens and Berthold Lubetkin, whose monographs are usually found side by side on alphabetical shelves, are household names, while there are many significant figures about whom no critical commentary has been written. In Richardson's case, an older generation can remember him as a public figure in the post-war years, while for others, his name may well have been forgotten. He belongs among the opponents of Modern architecture who suffered relative neglect from the specialised press during their later years, and is probably chiefly remembered for his defence of eighteenth-century standards. For some, opposition to Modernism is necessarily good, while for others it is the reverse, but it would diminish Richardson's significance to leave him for ever locked in such a conflict. Not all 'non-Modernist' architects necessarily reward much attention, but even Richardson's opponents would probably agree that he deserves reappraisal, in all his fields of endeavour, in order that a complete picture of architecture in the twentieth century can be created, in which such conflicts, if not resolved, can at least be productive of a more general understanding.

The listing of Bracken House, his building of 1954–9 for the *Financial Times* in Cannon Street, when under threat of demolition in 1987, was a token of widespread recognition of this late work, which even potentially hostile critics such as Ian Nairn had long recognised as exceptional among non-Modernist post-war designs, and in spite of the demonstration in front of the buildings in 1959 by the 'Anti-Uglies', an ad-hoc student protest group led by the pop artist Pauline Boty. Before Bracken House, no post-war buildings had been listed. In 1987 architectural taste was in a fluid condition, and Bracken House served, somewhat ironically, as a Trojan Horse for the listing of further post-war buildings, of which Richardson would, in most cases, strongly have disapproved. Nonetheless, the subsequent remodelling of this palazzo of pink brick and sandstone by Sir Michael Hopkins marked a moment of cross-over between the polarities of Modernism and its other. Describing his design for replacing the central section of Bracken House, Hopkins made reference to industrial buildings of the early nineteenth century, whose restrained toughness lay close to the root of Richardson's creativity as well. This was an interesting moment in which Hopkins overcame his generation's prejudice against traditional-looking details and realised that they could have expressive as well as practical benefits.

With only a trifling adjustment, Bracken House could be imagined as having been built by Richardson in the City of London forty years before its actual date. Like early buildings by Richardson and his first partner, C. Lovett Gill, it would then have seemed 'modern' for its time, although the word had a less definite meaning. The first fifteen years of Richardson's working life were a time when the technological and social changes of modernity, motor cars, aeroplanes, widespread industrial strikes, feminism and international finance, were being dramatically experienced and the opportunities to represent them through culture were being contested. A newspaper cutting from 1913, containing a plea by Richardson for Somerset House to be adopted as the seat of London University, has on the back an advertisement for HMV records of 'Tango – the world craze' and a report of the first public demonstration of a machine-gun mounted on a biplane.

Richardson's own architectural experiences as a pupil and assistant, before launching his practice with Gill in 1908, showed him several aspects of this social moment. He experienced three different kinds of architectural office with Evelyn Hellicar, Leonard Stokes and Frank Verity, which seem to have left him with an almost dualistic approach to architecture. The gentle Georgian revival of Hellicar could be linked to the Arts and Crafts Gothic of Stokes as representative of the careful and often nostalgic tendency of the time. Verity's influence pulled in a different direction, towards Paris and America, and to what passed as 'modern' in the early 1900s. As late as the 1950s, Richardson can be seen acting out these two roles, reflecting his first two masters in carefully restoring bomb-damaged buildings or creating new variants of old forms, as he did with the chapel at St Mary's College, Strawberry Hill, and in city buildings such as Bracken House, picking up the threads laid down by his work on Verity's Regent Street facades with an Edwardian panache. In his perceptive and timely article in the *Architectural Review* in 1965, based on an interview with Richardson two years earlier, Nicholas Taylor looked behind Richardson's persona of Georgian anachronism to imagine him as a young man growing up in, and thoroughly enjoying, a world of fast cars and mechanised construction.

All these influences were capable of being unified through the language of classicism, which Richardson's generation believed they had a special mission to rediscover. As he put it in a radio interview with Gilbert Harding in 1954, 'Some 50 years ago I realised that the Victorian had reached its limits, and that it was necessary to refocus attention on a good period in order to ensure intelligent evolution of a new manner.'[1] Thus new and old were seen as essentially unified, with a sense of cultural continuity that British architects felt had been preserved in France. Richardson claimed to have designed many of Verity's elevations, including the impressive facade of the Regent Street Polytechnic, derived from Paul Henri Nénot's Sorbonne, built in the 1890s with a grand order and a steep

figure 38
Frank T. Verity, elevation for Regent Street Polytechnic, 1910, designed by Albert Richardson in Verity's office

figure 39
Proposal for rebuilding Regent Street Quadrant, perspective by Richardson, 1912

roof. Such discipline of street architecture was new to London, but allowed for enough theatricality to satisfy the taste of the time. This building, and the contemporary King Edward VII Galleries of the British Museum by Sir John Burnet, contributed to a reaction against the loose, picturesque classicism of Norman Shaw, manifested simultaneously in Shaw's controversial Piccadilly Hotel at the other end of Regent Street.

Admiration of Norman Shaw was a condition of membership of the Edwardian architectural élite, as defined by figures such as Lutyens and Blomfield. Richardson, together with Charles Herbert Reilly and Stanley Adshead, his friends then teaching at Liverpool University, were among a younger generation outside this charmed circle who dared to criticise Shaw in public for the crude-

figure 40
Revised design for Swan and Edgar, Piccadilly Circus, 1914

figure 41
10 Berkeley Street, London W1, elevation

ness of some of his later work. Richardson made common cause with the shopkeepers of the Quadrant who opposed the extension of Shaw's designs on grounds of its commercial disadvantage, and the *Builder* magazine, then edited by the architect H.V. Lanchester, set up an architectural competition for an alternative scheme which Richardson & Gill won in 1912. But for the First World War, their design might have been built, instead of Sir Reginald Blomfield's 1920s reworking of Shaw. It was an attempt to adapt the character of the original Nash Quadrant to the larger scale of the rebuilding, slimming down the level of architectural ornament and relying more on small-scale detail and plain surface.

Commentators of the time recognised the competing claims of civic monumentality and commerce in the rebuilding of the Quadrant and Piccadilly Circus. Richardson and his contemporaries, newly enthused by the American 'City Beautiful' movement, tried to bridge these worlds, but Richardson, in particular, was able to give positive expression to the shops and their goods as an aspect of urban modernity that should be celebrated through appropriate architecture, rather than concealed. His revised design in 1914 for Swan and Edgar, at the southern termination of the Quadrant, shows the use of glass and steel to create 'a vast open bazaar' with a rooftop restaurant. The visual form of this elevation was a novel but harmonious assembly of classical precedents. He complained that London building regulations restricted experiments of this kind and forced architects to use excessive areas of masonry.

Richardson's orchestration of a publicity campaign around the Quadrant was almost as impressive as the design itself, and, in its way, an expression of modernity. Articles appeared in the *Daily Telegraph* and the *Pall Mall Gazette* as well as in the professional journals, proclaiming the scheme as a harbinger of public involvement in raising standards of civic design, mostly written (anonymously) by Richardson himself and illustrated with his fresh-looking line drawings. The word 'modern', still innocent of exclusive stylistic meaning, was freely used, and the text of a *Daily Telegraph* article of June 1, 1912, under the heading 'New

Materials and New Architecture', explains the value of reinforced concrete framing and painted stucco finishes.

Richardson was of the first generation of architects in Britain to practise from the outset with the steel frame, first employed in the Ritz Hotel in 1906. Shortly afterwards, reinforced concrete became another alternative to load-bearing construction. The architectural consequences of these major steps in the transformation of technique were discussed by some, such as W.R. Lethaby and Beresford Pite, in terms which can be related to the proto-modernism of Auguste Perret in France, but Edwardian architects assimilated them chiefly by a turn away from structural rationalism towards the vocabulary of Italian Mannerism (a term not then current), as can be seen in the work of Belcher & Joass and Charles Holden. Richardson's group of friends set themselves apart by preferring purity to conscious novelty, and refrained from architectural irony. The difference can be seen even in the 1930s when Charles Holden was composing London buildings, such as Senate House, as modelled masses while Richardson came closer to the expression of framed structure. He made a specialism of the design of street frontages early on, continuing the 'Neo-Grec' style of Verity's office into the two early residential buildings at Nos. 10 and 19 Berkeley Street, Mayfair. 'Neo-Grec' was the catch-phrase of the period 1908–12, referring to the eclectic 'modern' classicism of Paris from the 1840s, demonstrated most clearly in the Palais de Justice by J.L. Duc, a building about which Richardson wrote in the *Architectural Review* in 1913–14. This synthetic classicism, characterised by Portland stone facades with solid balcony brackets, swags of fruit and foliage and bands of guilloche around doorways, was a widely popular style which sadly produced very few buildings to inspire affection. It was satirised in a rhyme recalled by Arthur Davis, co-designer of the Ritz, in 1947:

Mutules in the cornice,
Acanthus round your door,
Small bars in the windows
Three feet from the floor.
Georgian in the country,
Neo-Grec in town,
That's the stuff to give them
If you seek renown.[2]

Neo-Grec could be seen as a hard-edged style filling the gap which, in several European cities, was occupied by the precursors of Modernism, such as the Schinkelesque Mannesman headquarters of Peter Behrens in Dusseldorf, 1910, the early works of Auguste Perret, the municipal projects of Tony Garnier in Lyon, and the work of Otto Wagner, an architect Richardson admired greatly, to the extent of keeping a book of Wagner's designs by his drawing board throughout his life. With its totally conventionalised ornament and absence of *facture* and truth to materials, Neo-Grec was at the opposite pole from Arts and Crafts and, as Simon Houfe explains in his essay in this catalogue, Richardson underwent a transformation from one set of values to the other during the early years of the century. The 'Pevsnerian' interpretation of Arts and Crafts as the precursor of Modernism requires that classicism should become at best a transitional stage, while for Richardson it was a central point to which everything else could be related. He increasingly saw classicism as inseparable from craftsmanship and proper handling of materials, although he rejected any idea that the materials could determine the design of the building without a conscious intervention by the architect.

As an architecture of rationalism and conventionality, classicism not only responded to modern forms of building construction, but presented an alternative to Art Nouveau for those who no longer believed in the need for a separate and novel 'style of the age'. It therefore represented in Richardson's career, as in many other architects', the rational aspect of Modernism without the avant-garde or consciously innovative. This classical movement of the early 1900s was widespread, from Heinrich Tessenow's faux-naif housing terraces in Dresden to Gunnar Asplund's Villa Snellman, from Auguste Perret's Théâtre des Champs Elysées to the early villas of Mies van der Rohe. If we consider the dates of birth of this sample of architects (1876, 1885, 1874, 1886), we find Richardson, born in 1880, generationally right in their midst. It was not a movement based on theory, but some of its intellectual grounding can be found in Herman Muthesius's short book, *Style Architecture and Building Art*, 1902, which sketches a version of 'the end of history', when styles cease to develop in the succession

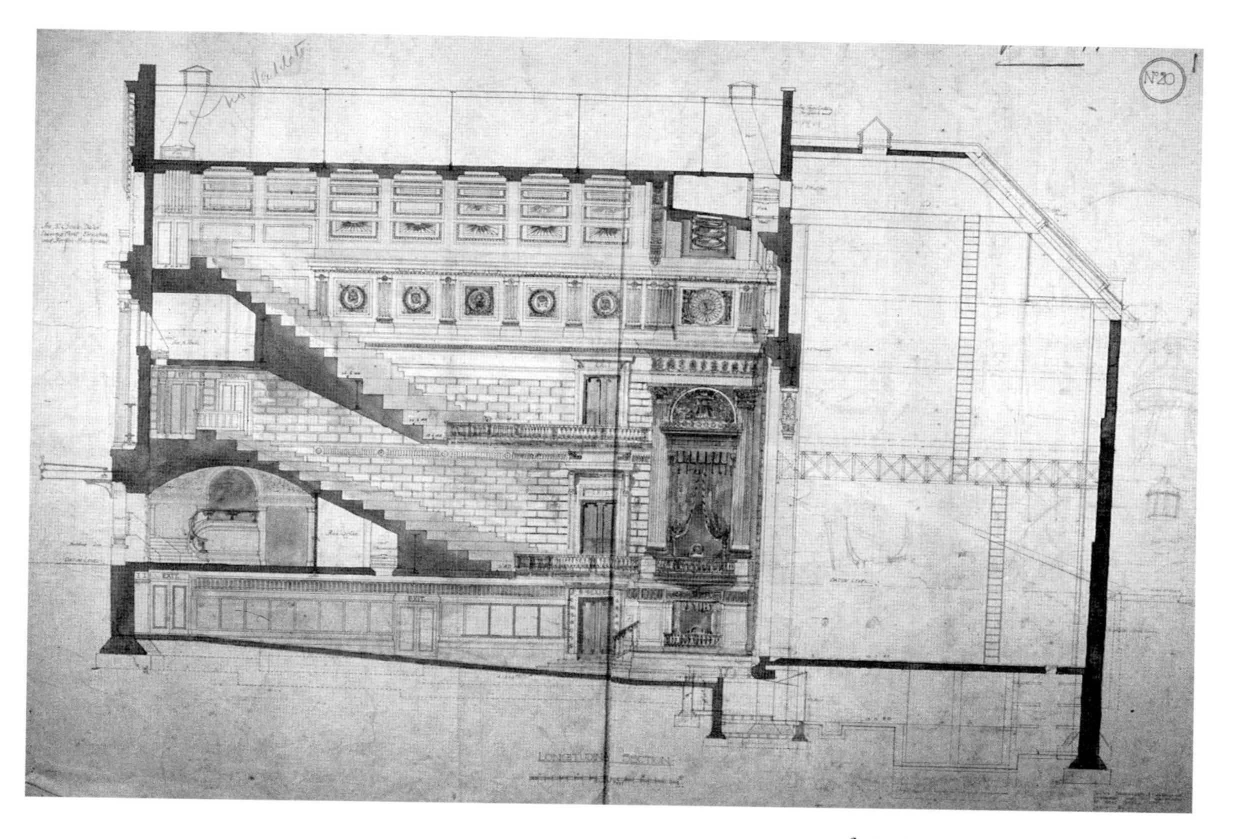

figure 42
Richardson & Gill with Horace Farquharson, New Theatre, Manchester, section, 1912

understood by historians, and architecture becomes a special aspect of the more generic activity of 'building art', a form of production suited to an industrial age. Significantly, Muthesius holds up the Biedermeyer style of provincial Germany around 1820 as a model for this new understanding of anonymous, normative design.

Richardson almost certainly knew nothing of Muthesius's book, and there was no equivalent in the architectural literature of England or America. Geoffrey Scott's *The Architecture of Humanism*, published in 1914, was the nearest equivalent, and a book which Richardson admired and recommended to anyone travelling to Italy. Scott also sought the universal in architecture through an abstracted understanding of classicism, and thus, as in Germany, conservatism and progressivism looked, for a time, very much the same. This changed, first in Germany with designs such as Walter Gropius's Fagus Factory of 1910, although Modernism's affinity with the period around 1800 formed many of its aesthetic principles. After the First World War, a complex combination of factors led to the development in Germany and elsewhere of what soon became recognised as 'Modern Architecture', the style of white walls and flat roofs which Richardson felt committed to oppose, yet the Czech architect Karel Honzik, writing in 1937, understood the interweaving of Classicism, Arts and Crafts and Modernism that made England a special case when he wrote that, 'the so-called English conservatism is an entirely specific compound in which not only the past but also the future is represented and – most surprising of all – in which many modern characteristics are preserved'.[3] Richardson was one of the first in Britain to use the term 'Modernism' in the discussion of architecture, in an unsigned editorial in the *Builder* in 1915, and continued the discussion into the 1920s.

Richardson's activities before 1914 corresponded closely to the programme outlined by Muthesius for reviewing the assumptions of architectural culture, displacing the romantic cult of individual 'genius' and originality in design in favour of more objective standards, which were recognised as having existed up until the 1830s; although in his lecture of 1912, 'The Academic in Architecture', he answered the critics of systematised design somewhat in the manner of Sir Joshua Reynolds, by proposing that 'the inventive faculty is strengthened by contact with tradition'.[4] Even in his more elaborate buildings, such as the New Theatre, Manchester, Richardson worked towards increasing simplicity. The façade, with its echoes of C.R. Cockerell and J.I. Hittorff, is an amalgam of 19th century public buildings, while the interior, in succession to the Scala Theatre, London, which Richardson had detailed in Verity's office, holds back from the full-blown vulgarity of Frank Matcham or Bertie Crewe. Perhaps more than any of his other early buildings, it is a built manifesto for the historical thesis of his book, *Monumental Classic Architecture.* The designs for the smaller Theatre Royal in Torquay of 1914, on the other hand, show Richardson working in a less eclectic manner, more appealing as a pastoral fantasy of recreating a kind of Regency theatre that never quite existed.

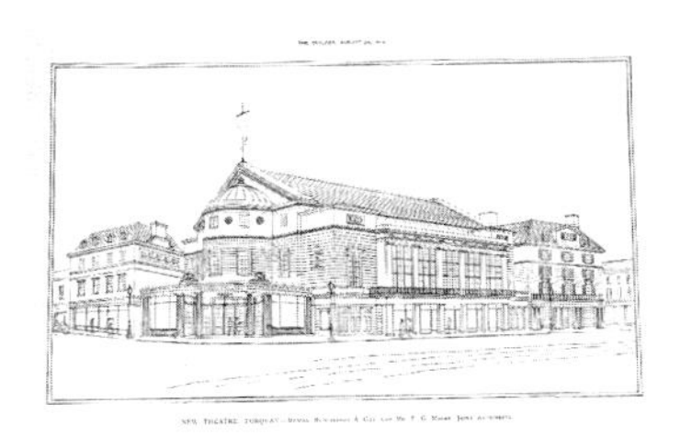

figure 43
Richardson & Gill with F.G. Moore, Theatre Royal, Torquay, 1914

Richardson's ambition to create a new form of civic architecture went well beyond even the achievement of the Manchester Theatre. It was a period of large-scale rethinking of London streetscape, goaded in part by the failure of new streets like Kingsway to reach expectations of quality. Richardson wrote in the *Builder* in June 1914 on 'The Spoiling of London'. The campaign was a group effort by like-minded architects and journalists. While much of the artistic effort of Edwardian England went into a search for essential qualities of Englishness, Richardson was the architect perhaps most concerned with constructing the essence of London and rediscovering the fabric of the pre-Victorian city with a view to harmonising future development.

Richardson and Gill's book, *London Houses 1660–1820*, published in 1911, proclaimed its novelty in representing the later part of the period for the virtue of its terraces, squares and ensembles, and upholding visual rather than sentimental or antiquarian values attaching to old buildings, much though Richardson valued these too. Edwardian classicists such as C.H. Reilly were inclined to condemn the Arts and Crafts movement as anti-urban. Richardson's ideal of urban domesticity in fine Georgian houses with back gardens, with harmonious public architecture, are much the same as C.R. Ashbee's when founding the Survey of London in 1896, or W.R. Lethaby's increasing concern with the appearance of towns in the 1900s. The architectural profession discovered town planning as an extension of their activities around 1910, and Richardson was foremost among those planning large-scale formal transformations of London, such as the scheme for a new St Paul's Bridge, one of three winners of a competition held in 1914. Without the First World War, this scheme, in addition to the Regent Street Quadrant, might have made Richardson's work more immediately recognisable. Whether its bombastic Beaux-Arts trappings would have been as likable in reality as the Quadrant promised to be is another question. Richardson never car-

figure 44
St Paul's Bridge, competition design, 1914

ried out work in this heroic mode, although many schemes, more or less real, were prepared. These included a new National Gallery, very American in style, and a similar proposal for the rebuilding of King's Cross Station. He even proposed skyscrapers for London in the style of pre-1914 New York examples.

GEORGIAN IN THE COUNTRY

Affection for the old and enthusiasm for the new were believed to be reconcilable, if only past and present mediocrity could be erased, yet that an inconsistency arose between Richardson's book and his architectural practice is evident when he praised 'the English principle of home life' against 'the erection of modern blocks of flats' such as he was building in Mayfair.[5] The idea of architectural preservation was strongly advocated in his book, well before the legal means of achieving it through listing were considered politically possible. In establishing his position in the period before 1914, one must allow for a tension between his willingness to welcome aspects of modernity in the design of commercial buildings and his depth of affection for a pre-industrial world.

Anxiety about modernity is, in its way, a significant aspect of the development of Modernism in Europe, so this should not be seen as a disqualifying factor on Richardson's part, rather as revealing his full engagement in the problems of his time. In Germany, Ferdinand Tonnies's *Gemeinschaft und Gesellschaft*, 1887, deplored the loss of the preindustrial society with its network of personal contacts, and inspired early German modernists to rebel against the physical structure of the industrial city and seek inspiration from the English Garden Cities and from older settlements. *London Houses 1660–1820* is, in its way, a work of social criticism from a period when the conflict of the new and old worlds already seemed imminent.

The rural counterpart to the urban progressive tendency in Richardson's early

figure 45
Richardson & Gill, Lodges at Princetown, Devon

figure 46
Tor Royal, Princetown, Devon, 1798, altered by Richardson & Gill, *c.*1913, drawing by Hanslip Fletcher

figure 47
Scheme for Hugh Town, St Mary's, Scilly Isles

career can be found in his work for the Duchy of Cornwall, in Devon, Cornwall and the Scilly Isles, from 1913 onwards. This was part of a scheme of regeneration of the Duchy's holdings under (Sir) Walter Peacock (1871–1956), who also commissioned Adshead and Ramsey to rebuild sections of the Duchy's Kennington estate and was inspired by Richardson's articles on 'The Empire Style in England' in 1911, beginning with the restoration of Tor Royal at Princetown in Devon, a house of the early 1800s, which was rebuilt by Richardson for the use of the Prince of Wales. The alterations to farmhouses and cottages which formed part of Richardson & Gill's work for the Duchy are comparable to the Kennington work in being virtually reproductions of early nineteenth-century style, with sophisticated small-scale details, like the 'Gothick' glazing of the lodges which made a formal entry to Princetown, based closely on the lodge to Tor Royal which Richardson illustrated in his book of 1924, *Regional Architecture in the West of England.* The young Prince was encouraged to take a personal interest in the developments, and visited the Scilly Isles, where, after the war, Richardson planned an ambitious formal development of terraced houses in Hugh Town, St Mary's, some parts of which were carried out, although not the main feature of a symmetrical grouping of terraces and flanking quadrants, centred on a domed and columned rotunda. His work on the Scillies in the early 1920s included houses which were flat-roofed for economy, although essentially Georgian in elevation, and bungalows built with a concrete frame. To see it illustrated

in the magazines around the time of the First World War is to suffer a shock at the plainness of it and the apparently deliberate avoidance of aestheticism by a designer who knew very well how to be charming. All this work represents the concept of 'Baukunst' described by Muthesius, with an added quality of regional character which Richardson was usually able to assimilate because of the suppression of individualism in his designs and his attention to the spirit of the place, signalled in its existing buildings.

Richardson seemed not to tire of building three-bay houses with hipped roofs

and a central porch. There are several versions of this design among the work for the Duchy, another built on a site adjoining his own property at Ampthill in 1920, and a variety of versions from after the Second World War, such as the house at Weston Patrick, Hampshire, or the Principal's Lodge at St. Hilda's College, Oxford. A suburban version was designed for a site in St John's Wood. Richardson's house of 1954, for J.P. White, owner of the Pyghtle Works, a high-quality joinery firm in Bedford, was published in *Country Life*, noting that this five-bay, substantial-looking house had been built within the restrictions of building licences. The publication produced a large number of requests for Richardson and Houfe to design similar houses.

The house at Sunninghill for General Sir Bruce Hamilton of 1914, the first substantial country house which Richardson designed, has an American colonial character with its high roof and regularity of fenestration which is striking in its deliberate understatement. He became skilled at adapting country houses, a line of work much in demand in the 1920s. Blue Hayes, Broadclyst, near Exeter, was given the addition of a rear wing in 1920, with a bow window and separate access to the garden. 'Goldings', near Loughton, Essex, consisted of a tidying-up and addition of a single-storey extension to the garden front, with bowed ends. Most of Richardson's domestic work was late Georgian in character, with the exception of his picture gallery for Lord Fairhaven at Anglesey Abbey, Cambridgeshire, which is based, perhaps less successfully, on Tudor motifs. Richardson also designed a house in the Argentine for Madame Cacano, the widow of the Argentine Ambassador, which was never built. This has a central villa with outbuildings forming a courtyard, all with deeply projecting eaves.

Richardson designed a number of rural housing schemes, including three in villages in West Suffolk, and housing in Old Warden, Bedfordshire, where the pairs of cottages are linked with low walls. A similar kind of composition was proposed for a suburban site at 34 Shakespeare Road, Bedford, with a more urban character. In Saunders Piece, Ampthill, Richardson grouped eight white-washed council houses round a green, which became a model for similar developments at Flitwick and Woburn. Like other architects of the time, such as Tayler & Green in Norfolk, he tried to modify the effect of disconnected houses in landscape, whose height was greater than older houses because of the minimum standards laid down by building regulations, by emphasising the horizontal, and providing linking elements and garden hedges.

At Stewartby, near Bedford, a model industrialist's village begun in the 1920s by Sir Malcolm Stewart, the owner of the local brickworks, Richardson added

figure 48
House in Argentine for Madame Cacano

figure 49
House at Weston Patrick, Hants, 1958

figure 50
Cottages at Old Warden, Bedfordshire, c.1946

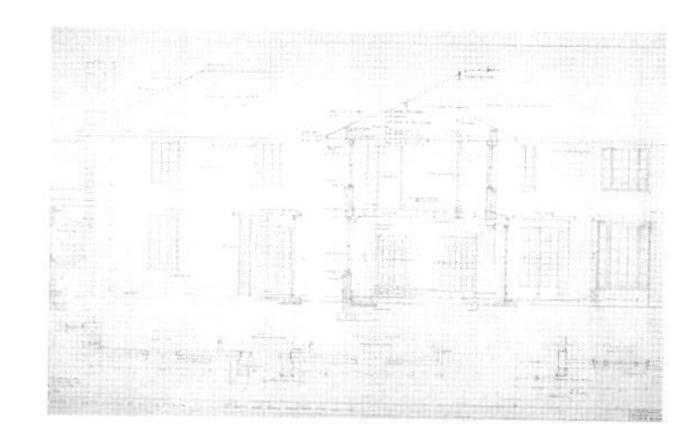

figure 51
Sir Malcolm Stewart Homes, Stewartby, Bedfordshire, 1955

figure 52
Sir Malcolm Stewart Homes, Stewartby, Bedfordshire, 1955

figure 53
Moorgate Hall, perspective

in 1955 a group of Old People's Homes to the existing group of buildings by Vincent Harris and Oswald P. Milne. This is on higher ground, away from the centre of the village, and includes one of Richardson's happiest inventions, a common-room in the form of a pavilion, with a concave copper roof and a slender colonnade all round, furnished with specially-made furniture by the Pyghtle Works.

OFFICE FACADES

As the memoirs of W.A. Downe indicate, the early years of the practice of Richardson & Gill depended largely on commissions for office and warehouse buildings in the City of London for the solicitors Herbert Reeves. The sequence of commissions continued into the early 1930s, and was succeeded by others of similar character. The first, designed before 1914 and completed in 1917, was Moorgate Hall, regrettably demolished in the 1980s, where Richardson's appreciation of the realities of commercial building, requiring letting units of flexible size, led him to treat the shops on the ground floor as a nearly continuous ribbon of glass, broken only by the double-height main door, in defiance of the conventional architectural wisdom that street facades should display their means of physical support through solid masonry piers. Richardson designed the upper part of the building in an architectural form of low relief, so that its apparent weight was diminished, in contrast to the designs of some of his contemporaries, such as Charles Holden, who were trying to create effects of mass.

There were other factors in this slimming down of the facade, however. Richardson's historical studies in these years had included Karl Friedrich Schinkel (subject of an article in the *Architectural Review* in 1912) and Alexander 'Greek' Thomson. Both offered models for the composition of facades of shallow depth, with a large area of window, in which aspects of vertical and horizontal modelling could be layered to create an overall composition. From Schinkel, probably, derives the vertical grouping of three windows within a flat wall-plane, repeated to make the main body of the building, with mezzanine storeys above and below. The seventh storey is set back, as the building regulations required, but the central five bays are brought forwards as an enriched pavilion. Although, as Nicholas Taylor was the first to point out in 1965, a partial precedent for this form of composition was given by Charles Barry's facade of 16–17 Pall Mall (1833–34, demolished 1913), Richardson seems to have made a synthesis of sources and produced a solution which, if not entirely original, had long been forgotten. C.H.

Reilly, writing in *Country Life* in 1925, gave Richardson the credit 'for first finding so simple and effective a method of decorating a long front'.[6]

Moorgate Hall had an exceptionally long frontage. The building at 45–53 Moorgate, 1921–23, had less central emphasis, partly to conceal the necessity of incorporating an existing right of way through the site with an inset entrance. In the upper part, alternating bays are enriched with console brackets and projecting hoods, crowned by a Greek key pattern cornice. In these buildings, the oddity of the 'Neo-Grec' of 1910 has been discarded and replaced by a more refined vocabulary of neoclassical detail.

The next important building in the sequence, Leith House, Gresham Street (1925–26) occupied, before its demolition, a curving site near Goldsmiths Hall in the City. The architectural character was more 'stripped' than its predecessors, probably reflecting Richardson's concern in the period 1923–26 with the meaning and possibilities of 'Modern architecture'. Richardson's period of reappraisal of his certainties has been obscured behind his later apparently uncomplicated assertion of classical superiority. A cartoon by H. de C. Hastings, later the proprietor and editor of the *Architects' Journal* and *Architectural Review*, published a cartoon to accompany the text of one of Richardson's lectures to the AA on 'The Renewal of Vitality in Building' in which the Professor stands in puzzlement as a ticker-tape comes down from above, reading, 'Stop press: message from Heaven (all quite new)' while in the waste paper basket are '18th century, My old friends Bill Chambers, Cockerell' etc.[7] As he said in another lecture in 1924, 'The present revolutionary thought ... aimed not so much at creating a new order of designing and fashioning, but a return to the structural principles of building, which alone could be used to express modern conditions.'[8] This, he said, had convinced him of the necessity of changing his ideas, revealing that the French tradition of academic planning might only be 'patterning on a grand scale' while industrial design, exemplified in the new tube train designs, provided an example of the alternative new approach.

figure 54
Alexander Thomson, Gordon Street warehouse, Glasgow, 1859–61, photo from Richardson's collection

figure 55
45–53 Moorgate, 1917–21

Richardson went on to explain the choice that he thought was available between 'blundering into novelty of form and massing by flights of fancy', and his preference for achieving style by continuity. C.H. Reilly, writing at the beginning of 1927, teased his friend and colleague that he had 'got religion', while feeling that the 'conversion' was shallow, which was partly true, and that Richardson's 'innate good taste and carefully acquired scholarship' showed

through the puritanism of the design of Leith House, which indeed had some low-relief enrichment on the piers at either end, capable of being cropped from a photograph.[9] Perhaps Richardson's 'Modernism' amounted to little more than catching up with the rest of Europe about ten years late, but the buildings show that the change was real. Ironically, the situation was reversed within a few years when Reilly became an advocate of Modernism and participated with William Crabtree in the design of Peter Jones, Sloane Square, 1935, whose curved frontage and vertical emphasis has at least a superficial resemblance to Leith House and retains many attributes of the Regency enthusiasm which Richardson and Reilly shared at the beginning of their careers.

Leith House is the only building by Richardson for which an engineer, Sven Bylander, is specifically credited. Bylander was a Swede who designed the steel work for Selfridges in 1911 and played an important if largely forgotten role in helping architects to adapt new building technology to their requirements. At Leith House, although the frame was steel, clad in Portland stone, the cornice was of reinforced concrete and constructed as part of the roof, which enabled it to achieve its thin profile, resembling designs by Auguste Perret or Otto Wagner more than anything previously designed by Richardson.

He was touched to receive a commendation from W.R. Lethaby, who was generally opposed to classicism as a revival style, while believing that some classical precedents could still be a creative stimulus. Lethaby wrote to Richardson on 19 February, 1926 to compliment him on a recent lecture and went on to praise Leith House: 'The tidy arranging of uprights, the well lighting, the reason of the whole thing, and then the piece of judgment in having the continuous band of window aloft to bind the verticals across seem to me admirable.'[10] Richardson was referring frequently to Lethaby's writings at this time, and it is not unreasonable to suppose that the work he was designing is a perfectly valid fulfilment of what Lethaby was asking for in architecture – a rational approach to materials without specific stylistic reference – even though Lethaby is more often associated with the origins of Modernism. F.R.S. Yorke and other architects in the Modern Movement in England in the 1930s felt that they too were fulfilling his suggestions, and there is no way of saying that one group is right and the other wrong.

More or less contemporary with Leith House were Stone House, 143 Bishopsgate and 65 Fenchurch Street, both with streamlined curved corners and the same basic elevational ordonnance derived from Moorgate Hall of a ground floor and mezzanine below a continuous balcony, surmounted by three equal storeys and a further mezzanine below a cornice, the whole topped by an attic. Neither of these has the distinction of St Margaret's House, Wells Street, designed in 1930 and completed in 1932. It is known that Richardson's personal level of involvement in the projects of the Richardson & Gill office was variable, and that Gill, while capable of learning from his partner, was never an inspired designer on his own. These are probably samples of his work.

Like Leith House, St Margaret's House, commissioned by Arthur Sanderson & Sons as part of their Berners Street premises but let as offices on completion, was more a warehouse than an office, a factor which may have influenced the unornamented character of the design. The groupings of windows within piers which are carried over the window heads in a single wall-plane is a continuation of the Moorgate Hall theme, but the contrast between the white brick of the wall and the black painted iron window-surrounds is more striking, and greater depth of wall is revealed, with each pier load carried down to the ground in this case. The deep set-back of the fifth storey is dramatic when seen obliquely, as is the curve of the copper roof, a pattern typical of Paris but almost unknown in London. Like many of Richardson's designs, St Margaret's House contains directions for an alternative street architecture for London. An aspect of the design particu-

figure 56
Leith House, Gresham Street, 1925–26

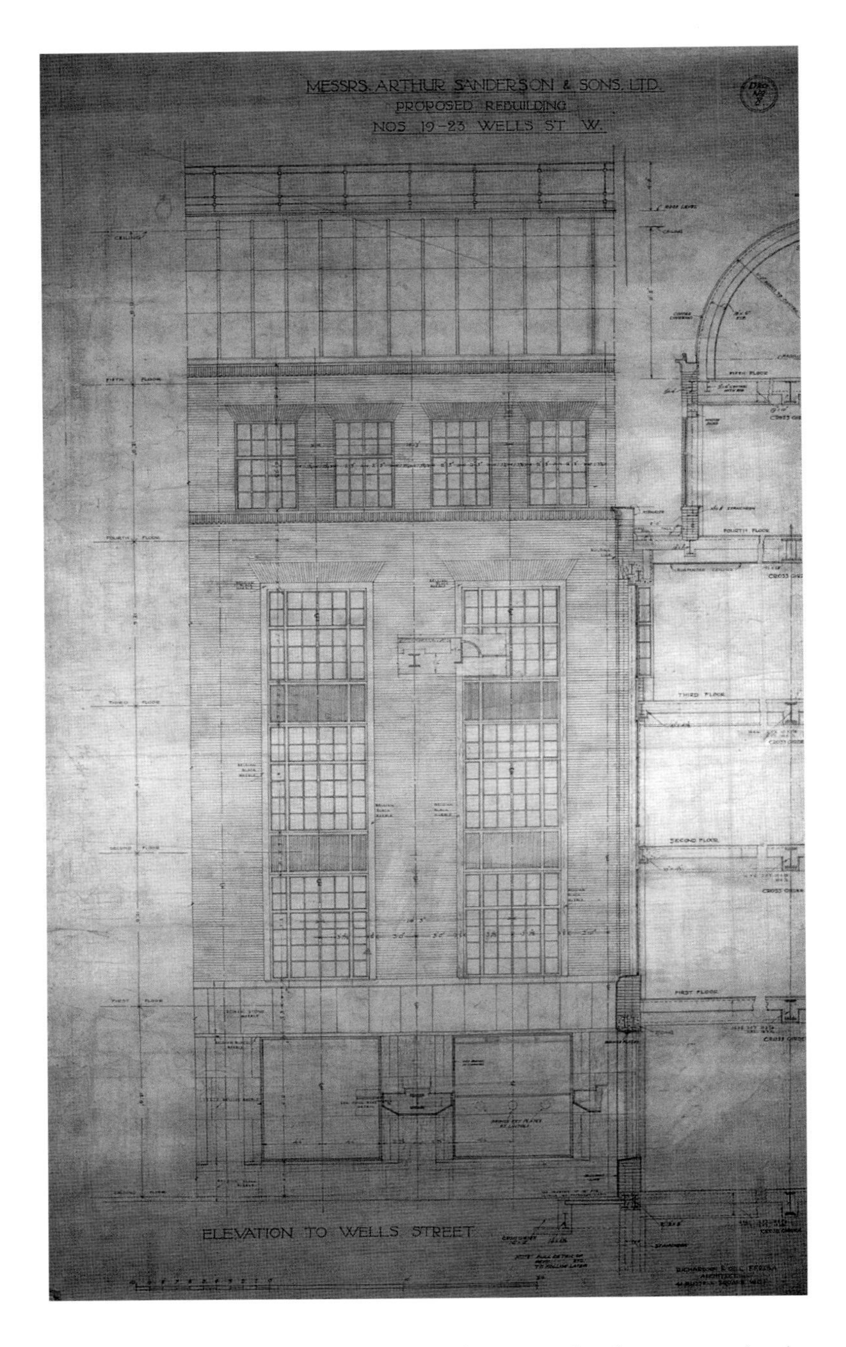

figure 57
St Margaret's House, Wells Street, 1930–31, elevation detail

figure 58
St Margaret's House, Wells Street, 1930–31

larly commended by the architect and teacher Howard Robertson was the absence of any 'end-stop' in the elevation, relying instead on the presence of the neighbouring buildings to provide a bracketing effect.

In a lecture of 1927, Richardson declared that 'Portland stone is a magnificent material for office buildings, for churches and monuments, but it is sadly out of place when attached to steel as a species of plating.'[11] He had used Portland stone at Leith House, but after this time often used brick for his London buildings, even though many architects continued to use Portland stone on steel framed buildings into the 1960s. St Margaret's House has specially-made 2 inch white bricks which are particularly appropriate for the design. The rear elevation is carried out in the highly glazed white bricks commonly used for London light-wells, with black brick sills, and an even more abstract effect, including a curved stair-tower with segmental windows. The building was awarded the RIBA London Architecture Medal in 1932 and still carries its plaque. An anonymous commentator in the *Architects' Journal*, aware that Richardson was already being seen as a joke figure, claimed that 'Professor Richardson is, in fact, not only an artist but a stylist; one of the few living English stylists of whom one can safely say that in whatever genre he builds the result will be coherent and satisfying.'[12]

Immediately after St Margaret's House, other architects, even naturally conservative ones such as H.S. Goodhart-Rendel, designed non-traditional street architecture in London, usually emphasising horizontality and extreme flatness. Richardson never stopped designing facades, whether for real buildings or as fantasy projects. In spite of the emphasis which he gave to plans in his statements about design theory, facades clearly interested him more than any other aspect of a building. He planned a series of six books on *Design in Civil Architecture*, with Hector Corfiato, of which only the first volume, 'Elevational Treatments', was produced, in 1948. It offered 'to link up experiences which extend over wide periods of time and outlook' and therefore help architects to avoid 'the danger of puerile copyism'. The text goes on to explain the importance of 'horizontal subdivisioning, vertical subdivisioning and balanced grouping of masses', but along with the necessary abstraction of architectural language, Richardson claimed here, as elsewhere, that symbolism could no longer be achieved by details alone, rather that 'character in civic building ... is concerned with those spiritual qualities of composition which convey outwardly the meaning and purpose for which the building is intended.'[13]

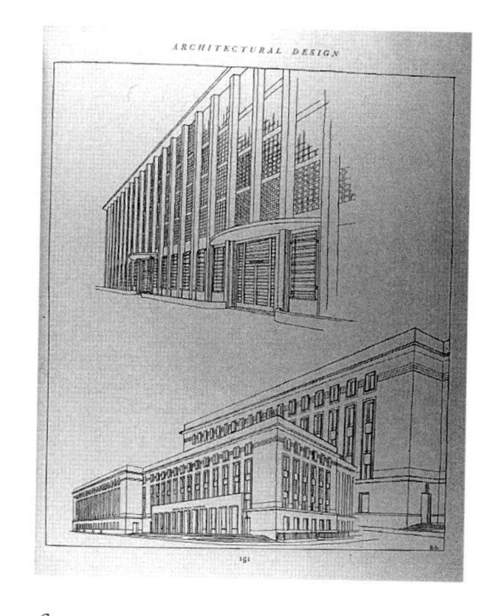

figure 59
Plate from Richardson and Corfiato, *Design in Civil Architecture*, 1948, illustrating Archives at Versailles and Post Office at Lyons

The examples given range from the Strozzi Palace to a school by Dudok in Hilversum. The majority of the later examples are typical of the 'stripped classic' style of the mid-twentieth century into which certain buildings by Richardson, such as Leith House, can be categorised. 'Stripped classic' can easily be recognised, but little effort has ever been made to understand it, partly because of the embarrassment caused by its adoption by the Nazi and Italian Fascist régimes (the Air Ministry in Berlin and Rome University are included, along with a number of 'Stalinist' buildings). 'Stripped' implies absence of details and mouldings which Richardson believed, at least in the mid-1920s, were better done without so that the essential qualities of structure and proportion could emerge. On the other hand, he was not dogmatic about this – allowing varying levels of detail to appear, depending on the use and status of the building concerned, nor did he feel it necessary to exclude detail on economic or functional grounds. The architects of the 1790s whom he particularly admired, such as Henry Holland, Samuel Wyatt and Robert Mylne, provided ample precedent for an essentially unornamented classicism. Part of the argument conducted by Richardson and his colleagues in the Edwardian period had been intended to ensure that ornament was beautiful and meaningful, while adapting the classical language to a larger scale of framed structure.

'Stripped classical' readily assumes the appearance of a half-way house on the road to Modernism, and hence implies a failure to finish the journey. This is a teleology that Richardson would have rejected, but it makes judgement of his later buildings more difficult. The Chancery Lane Safe Deposit, for example, is a dull building, although it has an overall character in its massing which distinguishes it from similar-looking 'Lessor Blocks' of the late 1940s, and just enough distinction around its entrance door to lift it from mediocrity. Richardson's additions to Trinity House, Tower Hill are inflected by the original Samuel Wyatt building, and complement it beautifully. His office block to the rear, Woodruff House, now demolished, needed to be dull in order not to upstage the original, but displayed the virtue of control. A similar playing-down can still be seen in Stone's Chop House, 1963, with its tight brickwork and stone dressings and chamfered corners, each containing a flattened urn.

The Associated Electrical Industries building in Grosvenor Place, completed in 1959, is, in some respects, the most anomalous of Richardson's post-war works, partly in its large scale and partly in its apparently complete disconnection from the other architecture of its time. It is evidently at odds with Modernism, but when compared to other semi-traditional headquarters buildings of this date, such as Howard Robertson's Shell Centre or Charles Holden's General Electric Building in Aldwych, it displays a confidence and competence they lack, and cannot be condemned in the terms of weakness and tiredness usually reserved for these late works of their authors. It is not helped by facing north-eastwards across a busy road, and thus not often being seen with sun on its main elevation, yet it has unusually lively sculpture by Maurice Lambert, with bronze terminals on the end pavilions. Would one desire it richer or plainer? Taller or shorter? The use of Portland stone for the whole of the exterior justifies Richardson's earlier suspicion of this material for framed buildings and probably contributes something to the sense of monotony, which perhaps also derives from the impenetrability and lack of visual transparency of the frontage. The Modern Movement tried to reconfigure the office building so that it effectively ceased to have facades, but post-modernism has restored the *status-quo ante*, without recovering the design skill necessary to implement it. To design more appealing elevations than those of AEI would be quite possible, but recent attempts, including a building on the site immediately to the south, show how far this is from being achieved.

To improve on the elevations of Bracken House, however, would be more difficult. This headquarters for the *Financial Times* suffers from some of the same problems of orientation as AEI, facing almost due north, although its eastern and southern elevations were treated as being wellnigh equally important, and the chamfered corners help to maintain the feeling of unity in the whole block. As originally built, Bracken House had the printing works occupying the central portion of the site, with two office wings acting like bookends. Richardson based

figure 60
Chancery Lane Safe Deposit, 1947–53

figure 61
Trinity House, Tower Hill, original building by Samuel Wyatt, 1793–6, restoration by Richardson & Houfe with additions, 1950–53

figure 62
Trinity House, elevation

figure 63
Stone's Chop House, Panton Street, elevation drawn by S.P.A. Holland, exhibited Royal Academy, 1955

figure 64
Associated Electrical Industries, sketch design

figure 65
Associated Electrical Industries, Grosvenor Place, 1956

the relationship of wings and centre in part on the Palazzo Carignani in Turin, which he sketched on a holiday in the early 1950s, although what in the case of the palazzo was the front became at Bracken House the side elevation. The reconstruction by Michael Hopkins and Partners, 1987–91, puts the main entrance back into the position of this original, while losing the sense of a deep recession between the 'wings'.

A number of factors seem to contribute to the success of Bracken House, which was deemed in 1964 by Ian Nairn to be 'a serious and sincere building, a real attempt to adapt and extend eighteenth-century language to modern conditions'.[14] The materials, pink brick and Hollington sandstone, were selected to mirror the *Financial Times*'s distinctive pink paper. They achieve a successful contrast with the green copper of the roof, while blending with the bronze of the windows. The main elements of the design are plain, as in Leith House, but there is more pleasure to be had in the smaller details, like the projecting windows of the ground floor with their concave corners and colonettes, the oak-leaf guilloche around the main door, the lanterns over the corner entrances and, most conspicuous of all, the Astrological Clock, centred on the face of the sun, unmistakably that of Brendan Bracken's friend and patron, Sir Winston Churchill. In the attic storey, the use of prismatic glass blocks between the windows adds sparkle and an element of surprise. While the north block has chamfered angles, the south block, originally called St Clement's Press, has turrets part buried in the wall to get round two awkward corners.

clockwise from top right · figure 66
Bracken House, 1955–9, sketches of elevation and clock

figure 67
Bracken House, perspective drawn by E.A.S. Houfe, exhibited Royal Academy, 1954

figure 68
Bracken House (St Clement's Press)

figure 69
Bracken House, detail of Astrological Clock, modelled by Philip Bentham with sun in the form of Sir Winston Churchill's face

When Bracken House was under threat of demolition in 1986, Sir John Summerson, who studied architecture at the Bartlett School under Richardson in the 1920s and admitted to finding the building 'constipated' when new, offered a reappraisal of the building to Gavin Stamp for use in the Thirties Society's campaign for its listing, having grown to appreciate it: 'Richardson's City architecture was the best of its time. His Moorgate Hall (1913–17), 47–57 Gresham Street and Sanderson's building in Wells Street, W1 (1930–32) lead up to Bracken House (1955–58), the most ambitious of the series. Direct and severe, it is also firmly modelled and shows the hand of a dedicated classicist. It is in the great line of City architecture going back to Gibson and Somers Clark (whose surviving City buildings are listed) and P.C. Hardwick and Cockerell (whose buildings have not survived). Richardson leaves out the columns but has the true sense of profile and light and shade. A very distinguished work.'[15]

CHURCH BUILDING

Richardson built two completely new churches and a college chapel and made competition designs for the cathedrals at Guildford and Coventry. In addition, without ever becoming a specialist in ecclesiastical work, he carried out repairs and rebuildings at a number of ancient churches, rebuilt important churches by Wren and Hawksmoor after bombing and contributed to the fittings of York Minster, Ripon Cathedral and Westminster Abbey.

figure 70
Holy Cross, Greenford, recent photo of interior

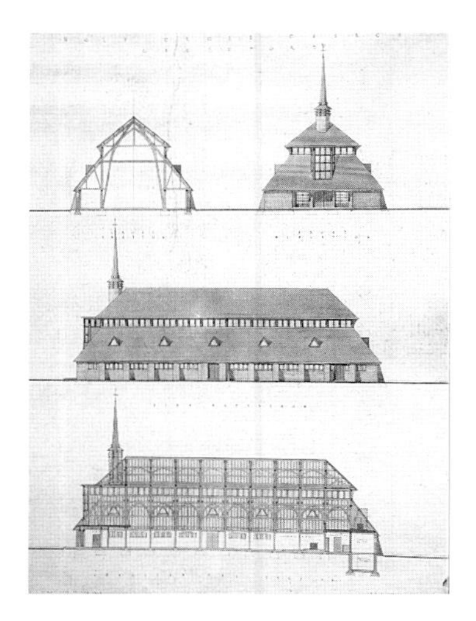

figure 71
St Christopher, Round Green, Luton, 1937 (section drawing)

figure 72
Holy Cross Greenford, 1939–42

The two new churches, Holy Cross, Greenford and St Christopher, Round Green, Luton, are related designs, based on a timber truss structure composed of interlocking straight members, creating a low-eaved profile on the exterior. Both churches had a long gestation and went through several design stages, the Luton church beginning with a stepped brick west elevation in 1930, the Greenford church, represented in a model, having a much more obviously Gothic quality externally. In both cases, the simplifications were advantageous, particularly in the case of Greenford, where the length of the single nave creates an impressive lattice-effect of timber, both complex and unfussy. This struck Ian Nairn who wrote 'the outside looks dowdy, but the inside is truly modern in the sense that it does not look over its shoulder at all, and simply does what it has to do'.[16]

Richardson's design for Guildford Cathedral is an attempt to create a centralised liturgical space using the language of Gothic. It is more full-blooded and adventurous than the winning design by Sir Edward Maufe, but it is hard to imagine it as a finished building by Richardson. Perhaps it would have undergone a similar process of refinement as the churches did. The design for Coventry he treated in a calmer manner, enforced, perhaps, by the competition requirement for outline drawings only. It is 'stripped Gothic', resembling the chapel at St Mary's College, Strawberry Hill, which Richardson & Houfe completed in 1964. In its original conception around 1946, this had been fully Gothic, but turned into a tall brick structure reminiscent, as with many mid-century churches in England, of Albi Cathedral. Richardson's opportunity to design a classical church came late in his career, with the completion of St Martin's, Knebworth, a church begun by Sir Edwin Lutyens for his wife's family, the Lyttons. Richardson gave it a broad-eaved west front of Tuscan character with a cupola, not attempting to compete with Lutyens's small-scale mannerist heroics on the inside.

In his restorations and repairs, Richardson worked closely with the Society for the Protection of Ancient Buildings. His work at St Mary's, Shelton, Bedfordshire in 1931 was so unobtrusive that Sir Nikolaus Pevsner commented, 'wonderfully unrestored inside'.[17] The rebuilding of St Mary's, Eaton Socon, following

anticlockwise from top left

figure 73
Guildford Cathedral, competition design, 1931

figure 74
Coventry Cathedral, competition design, 1951

figure 75
St Mary's College, Strawberry Hill, Middlesex, chapel, 1960–64

its almost complete destruction by fire, was a more radical operation and turned Richardson's attention to the problem of declining skills in the building crafts. His response was to form the Honourable Company of Craftsmen in 1932–33, a venture which was well-supported but never followed through. In this enterprise, and in his increasing body of writing on craftsmanship, Richardson showed his response to the changing world around him and the intensity with which his imagination worked through physical objects, both old and new. The fear about the decline of craftsmanship was justified, and the position appeared to get progressively worse after the war, although there were sufficient skills available for the restoration of bombed churches and other buildings after the war. Many older or more traditionally-minded architects found an outlet for their talents in this area of work, including W. Curtis Green, Stephen Dykes Bower, Marshall Sisson and H.S. Goodhart-Rendel. Richardson's work stands well in this company and his restorations of St James's, Piccadilly and St Alfege, Greenwich are not only accurate and accomplished, but contrive also to introduce some genuine Georgian panache in the restoration of the trompe l'oeuil painted decoration and the recarving of the pulpit at Greenwich. His provision of low-level standard lamps among the pews at St James's, Piccadilly was criticised by Pevsner, on the grounds of being neither strictly period nor modern. They are, nonetheless, among the most practical forms of lighting for a congregation, leaving the upper part of the church unaffected by suspended fittings.

clockwise from top left

figure 76
St Martin, Knebworth, completion of church of 1914 by Sir Edwin Lutyens, 1963–4

figure 77
St Mary, Eaton Socon, Huntingdonshire, restoration after fire, 1932

figure 78
Eaton Socon, corbel carved by Percy Bentham representing himself and Richardson with a model of the church

BUILDINGS IN A BUCOLIC LANDSCAPE

Richardson's nostalgia for the eighteenth-century way of life affected his practice as an architect. 'Bucolic' means 'rural, rustic or countrified', qualities which Richardson appreciated in a moral sense as well as a pictorial one, as indicative

figure 79
Sir Christopher Wren (1632–1723), St James, Piccadilly, 1675–1710, restoration after bomb damage, 1947–54

figure 80
Nicholas Hawksmoor (*c.*1661–1736), St Alfege, Greenwich, 1712–14, restoration after bomb damage, completed 1963.

of a greater connection with reality than the modern civilisation of cities. Like Ferdinand Tonnies in the 1880s, he thought that a small country town offered an ideal scale for living, between the isolation of the country and the impersonality of the great city. Richardson wrote numerous articles on such towns in the architectural magazines during and after the First World War, and enjoyed the motor car because of the way, in its early years, in which it revived the life of old coaching inns which had been abandoned because of the railways. His nostalgia was shared by authors like George Sturt whose book, *The Wheelwright's Shop*, 1923, described the dying out of a rural craft in the Surrey town of Farnham, and became the basis for a critique of mass culture by F.R. Leavis and Denys

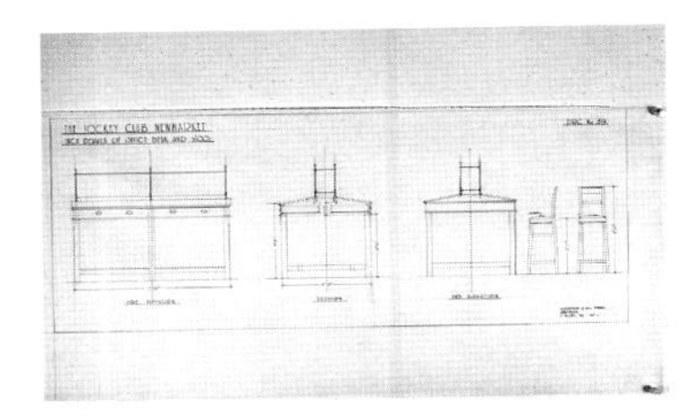

figure 81
Jockey Club, detail of furniture

figure 82
Jockey Club, Newmarket, Suffolk, perspective drawn by Albert Richardson, 1934

figure 83
Town Hall, Dulverton, Somerset, perspective drawn by Albert Richardson, 1927

Thompson in the 1930s. Writers like H.J. Massingham deplored the dying away of a generation of country people who possessed their own cultural forms, often of great beauty. Richardson's response was partly to collect old objects and re-enact scenes with them, but in a more practical way to give his buildings qualities of appropriateness to their setting. He also enjoyed the quality of exchange between the poles of town and country, when a sophisticated example of architecture, like his own Avenue House, was found in a country town, or an unexpected piece of rurality in the city, like the old lavender seller in Piccadilly whom he supported and patronised in the 1950s.

Richardson was also a pioneer in developing the concept of regionalism in architecture through his book *Regional Architecture of the West of England*, 1924. The concept itself was well established during the Arts and Crafts Movement, but Richardson brought to it a new sophistication in showing how the buildings of his favourite period, from 1760 to 1830, while reflecting a sophisticated metropolitan style, were also subject to regional variations in a kind of cross-breeding with older local traditions, often based on climate and materials.

The Jockey Club, Newmarket, which Richardson rebuilt in the middle years of the 1930s, is a prime example of the pleasure to be had from playing on the sense of regionalism and conscious evocation of the past. The High Street in Newmarket, where the pre-existing, rambling and ad-hoc buildings of the club stood, was the kind of scene Richardson liked to depict in his fantasy drawings of this period. He created a building with a generous street presence which avoids being a precise imitation of a Georgian building (at least, to the eye of a well-informed beholder), while being much better detailed than almost any other 'Neo-Georgian' architect of the period could have achieved. The sense of quality and detail carries through the ironwork, furniture and fittings and belongs properly to the world of horses and dogs, who do not understand Modernism.

Richardson depicted the Jockey Club with eighteenth-century figures in front, and drew the Town Hall at Dulverton, Somerset, in the same manner. This much simpler commission has the same quality of appropriateness, although consisting only of the addition of paired flights of steps up to a new doorway on the first floor of an existing building, supported on a stone arch. Most of the many architects practising in the Georgian manner in the inter-war period would have misjudged the mood of the place in some way. Richardson's little feat of structural bravura has a quality of authenticity that perhaps only Clough Williams-Ellis might have equalled.

These designs are far removed from the anxiety about Modernism which was a fruitful source for Richardson's City buildings, yet because of the shared basis of an underlying formal language of classicism, they are not wholly disconnected, just more relaxed about playing with time and place.

figure 84
Marshall Sisson (1897–1978). Study of the Orders, first year drawing at Bartlett School, 1920

figure 85
Marshall Sisson (1897–1978). Study for Rome Scholarship in Architecture, 1924

RICHARDSON AND EDUCATION

A significant part of Richardson's time was taken in teaching. He held the Professorship at the Bartlett School for 27 years, entering on the crest of the wave of Beaux-Arts enthusiasm and leaving when his insistence on graphic skills, simple graded design problems and relatively standard solutions was already under suspicion. A number of distinguished pupils emerged from the Bartlett, but of the names that are remembered, none followed their master's teaching literally. Marshall Sisson, winner of the Henry Jarvis studentship at the British School at Rome in 1928 built several flat-roofed houses in the early 1930s before reverting to classicism. Amyas Connell, who came to the Bartlett from New Zealand and won the Rome Prize itself in 1926, was commissioned by Bernard Ashmole to build 'High and Over' at Amersham in 1929, one of the first Modern Movement houses in England. He continued to design skilful but adventurous buildings through the 1930s with his partners Basil Ward (another Bartlett and Rome student) and Colin Lucas. John Summerson became a journalist and historian who gave to Richardson's discoveries in the English classical tradition the factual and speculative basis of a professional historian. He also promoted modernism and was ambivalent about the retention of old buildings. Colonel Richard Seifert, a student at the Bartlett in the period around 1930, demonstrated a different form of architectural modernism in a 'commercial' practice that dealt with design problems similar to those of Richardson & Gill

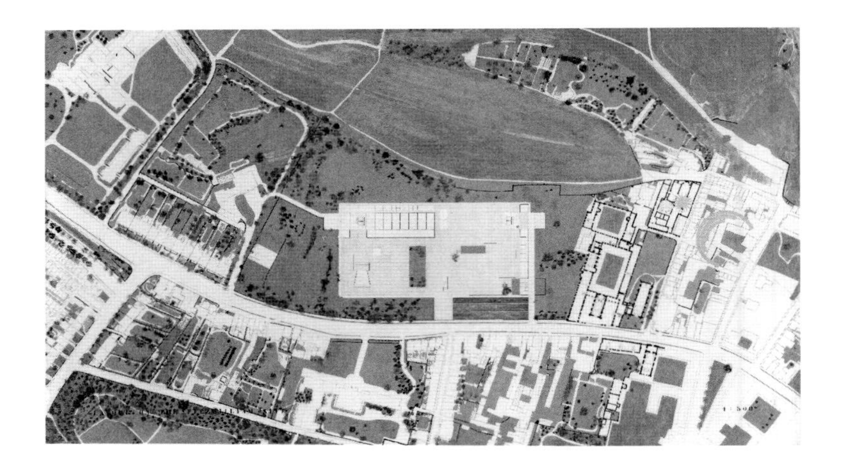

figure 86
Peter Smithson (b.1923) 'An Art Museum for a University Town', Royal Academy Grand Prize design, 1949 perspective with collage.

figure 87
Peter Smithson (b.1923) 'An Art Museum for a University Town', Royal Academy Grand Prize design, 1949, site plan

in their early years. On the other hand, Eric Houfe, who became Richardson's son-in-law and post-war architectural partner, was a Bartlett Graduate, as were Sam Holland and Ross Britain, two of the other mainstays of the post-war practice.

Richardson's chief teaching colleague in his early years was Arthur Stratton, a writer on English houses and author of *Elements of Form and Design in Classic Architecture*, 1925. From 1923, Hector Corfiato (1893–1963), a Maltese former student at the Ecole des Beaux-Arts, was an important staff member, who succeeded Richardson as professor in 1946, before being forcibly retired in 1961 in what was virtually a modernist 'coup'. Corfiato probably encouraged a more stripped classical manner in the school, but this was not incompatible with Richardson's beliefs.

In a radio debate in 1949, Richardson stated his belief that ability to draw should be the foundation of an architect's skill: 'An architect like a musician or a painter must be born. Training is merely the surface polishing of the diamond. The discovery of latent architect's genius ... is the duty of the teacher and the teacher must be an architect.' Some students, such as Louis Osman, 1931–35, also attended drawing classes at the Slade School, which occupied adjoining premises at University College, while Slade students such as Rex Whistler acknowledged the benefits of Richardson's knowledge of classical buildings. Anecdotes necessarily concentrate on what Richardson said to his students, but he also understood the value of not speaking, stating that 'the great thing is never to attempt to teach, remain silent, and you can draw ideas from your pupil. ... Encourage, and at the right moment they'll catch fire ...'[18]

Richardson's personal performance as a lecturer, drawing diagrams of buildings with both hands as well as showing glass slides with his own drawings made directly onto them, was the aspect of his teaching remembered and admired by all who witnessed it. Students from the Architectural Association would go the few hundred yards up Gower Street to witness the lectures, but when John Brandon-Jones, in the 1920s, complained to Howard Robertson, the Principal of the AA, about some aspect of his course and was offered the suggestion of going permanently to the Bartlett, the implication was that the AA would always have the edge on independent thinking and enterprise. Raymond Erith (1903–74) another AA graduate, was disillusioned by Modernism in the 1930s but felt that the elder generation of traditionalists were too intellectually weak to make their case properly. If classicism was to flourish, it needed to be more resilient and imaginative, less formulaic and polite. The book *The Art of Architecture* which Richardson wrote with Corfiato in 1938 shows how the classical diet was not exclusive (even the De La Warr Pavilion, Bexhill-on-Sea by Mendelsohn and

Chermayeff is illustrated), but reveals the tendency to rely on formal solutions to problems which young architects by this time believed required a more holistic approach through environmental design. Leo de Syllas, who left the Bartlett after his third year and went to the AA, becoming an editor of the radical student magazine *Focus* in 1938–39, exemplifies the way that criticism of Richardson's teaching approach went beyond oppositions of styles.

A lesser-known coda to his main teaching career was the reopening of the Royal Academy Architecture School in 1947. This had been discussed among the architect academicians during the war as a means of countering the tendency of modernism, and Vincent Harris provided an endowment in the form of rent from his property at 19 West Eaton Place. The mission, announced in the RA Annual Report for 1945, was 'the cultivation of quality in Architecture, through the study of the finest examples from the past, as a means to an end, and not as an end in itself'. An announcement in *The Times* on 17 December, 1946 called for students to participate in a one-year full-time graduate course, in place of the evening class in architecture which had run from 1870 until 1939, with gradually diminishing prestige. There would be a Grand Prize for design every year, and it was hoped that 'every student leaving the School will go forth properly equipped for the great work of reconstruction to be done in the coming years both at home and overseas'. Richardson took over the Professorship of Architecture (in abeyance since 1911) and offered his services free as a teacher, calling into the school once or twice a week, aided by his former pupil Marshall Sisson, who was Surveyor of the Academy and Master of the Architecture School.

The recruitment of students was a problem at the start that was never overcome. Only two remained from an initial intake of seven for the first year. In 1949, there were six, although Richardson's lectures on architectural history, similar to those given at the Bartlett, were attended by painting and sculpture students as well and popular. Surprisingly, one of the students in 1949 was Peter Smithson, who had graduated from Durham University (the course actually held in Newcastle) and had an ex-serviceman's grant to spend on a further year's training.[19] He wanted to come to London and spent much time looking at and drawing the classical churches and other buildings, such as Somerset House, which Richardson recommended. He was fascinated by the oddity of the course and its opposition to his own ideas, thinking that 'if one is antagonistic to classicism as an educational method, it would be useful to know as much as possible about classicism'. Richardson recognised his ability and they respected each other. Richardson gave Peter and Alison Smithson a set of silver teaspoons when they married during the year. Smithson felt, however, that he had merely exchanged a quasi-modernist formalism, as taught at Durham, for another – 'In today's terms, you'd call it general eclecticism', and that there was nothing strong enough to fight against. Having just discovered Philip Johnson's book on Mies van der Rohe, he submitted a completely Miesian scheme for the 1949 Grand Prize, the brief for which was a University museum on the site of the Fitzwilliam in Cambridge. According to Simon Houfe, Richardson praised Smithson's plan, which was certainly drawn to the required graphic standard. The Annual Report for 1949 noted that 'one or two of the students have very decided views on modern architecture and, although interested in the teaching, preferred to follow current fashions. This was particularly the case with Mr Smithson.' The Annual Report for the following year contained the information that 'One student has recently been awarded the First Prize in a Public Competition [Hunstanton School] and attributes his success to the training he received at the Royal Academy.'

After this, the Academy Architecture School went up slightly in numbers (fourteen in 1952) but then down to two again in 1956, one of whom, David Ottewill, was an assistant in Richardson's office, before being closed the following year. Surviving drawings in the Royal Academy Library show a lack of excitement, apparent in rather blank elevations and large symmetrical plan layouts. It is hard to see how this work could ever have achieved Richardson's initial intention of revitalising post-war planning for reconstruction.

During all stages of his teaching career, Richardson's bubble of enthusiasm carried his students along but it was not underpinned by the kind of analytical approach to classicism which is now common even in 'modern' schools of architecture. Joseph Rykwert recalls an occasion when Richardson chaired a lecture by Rudolf Wittkower, based on his book *Architectural Principles in the Age of Humanism*, which was Peter Smithson's other great discovery in 1949. Richardson was simply unable to acknowledge or comprehend the depth that Wittkower's researches added to the understanding of classicism and the way in which they supported many of his own criticisms of modernism as a shallow materialist theory of architecture.

GRAND DESIGNS AND CIVIC IMPROVEMENTS

The competition designs for the Regent Street Quadrant in 1912 and St Paul's Bridge were among the first of many such schemes by Richardson for large scale improvements of streetscape and planning. Others included the rebuilding of Euston Station and the National Gallery, both in Beaux-Arts style. Thinking beyond the individual building to the wider environment was one of his generation's contributions to architectural practice which was carried forward by the modernists, often without acknowledgment that they had such predecessors. This change towards a social concern for the totality of a street, town, city or whole country caused high hopes and frustrations, particularly when, during the 1920s, the forces of development were attacking the countryside. Richardson

top right · figure 88
Scheme for rebuilding of Euston Station, 1942

figure 89
Sketch for St Paul's Cathedral precinct, 1955

figure 90
Sketch for St Paul's Cathdral precinct, 1955

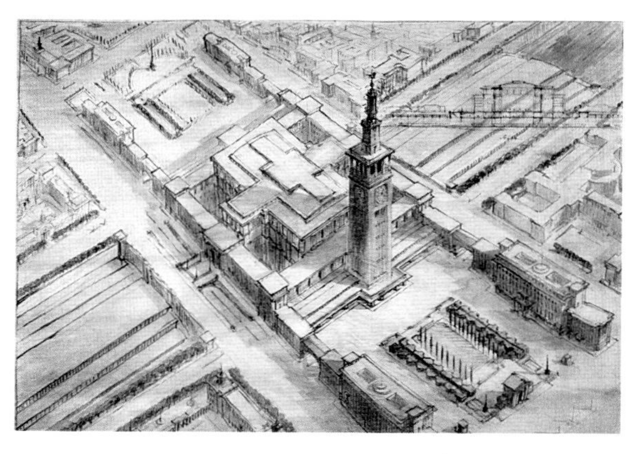

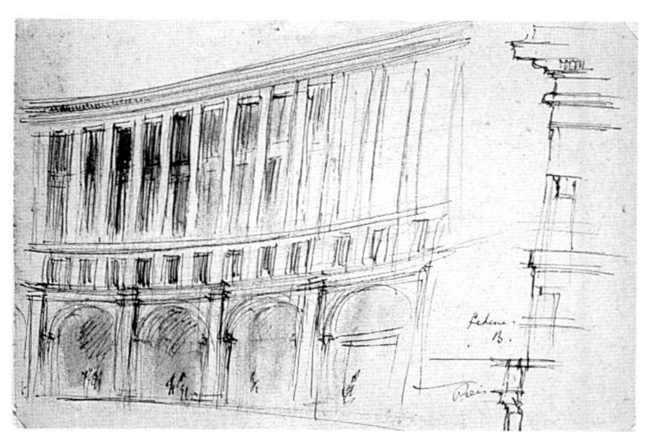

lectured extensively on issues of housing the expanding population and regenerating inner cities by converting Georgian houses to flats, displaying an almost poetic understanding of the pressures of social aspiration that caused demographic change and left fine buildings abandoned in their wake. Although he was prepared to admit that fantasy schemes, such as he liked to dream up, lacked the virtue imparted by realistic conditions, he drew up a design in 1940 for the rebuilding of Euston and St Pancras Stations (a real scheme proposed by the LMS Railway), including a skyscraper of pre-1914 New York style, like one that Richardson had published as a scheme for enlarging the Bank of England in 1922.

Richardson was one of the group of architect members of the Royal Academy who worked on the RA Plan for London in 1942, devising a string of grand buildings on the South Bank. He avoided the dullness which afflicted some of the other proposals, but also revealed an unresolved dichotomy between his love of the intricacy of old London, as captured in Hanslip Fletcher's drawings, and the desire to make formal vistas for the benefit of traffic circulation, including the area around St Paul's Cathedral. In 1955 the new Minister of Housing, Duncan Sandys, appointed Sir William Holford as a planning consultant for this area and Richardson, then President of the Royal Academy, was invited to join an advisory committee for the Minister. He used the opportunity to advocate a formal classical solution and, as Holford's biographers write, 'He and the Minister spent considerable time with a large-scale wooden model of St Paul's which Sandys had in his office, using wooden bricks to experiment with different forms of enclosure.'[20] Sandys was convinced by Richardson's proposal for a hemicycle facing the west end, broken in the centre for the approach via Ludgate Hill, which he explained in a broadcast as rivalling those of Bernini at St Peter's. 'Think what this would mean to the city. Think of the effects of light and shade, of the increased vistas.'[21] Holford felt constrained to develop this scheme further, although he did not feel convinced by it. Eventually, a letter from John Summerson on 8 November caused him to lose faith in its possibilities, since, as Summerson expressed it, 'a formal object situated *within* that throw [or 'psychological orbit' of the cathedral] but not touching its limits may be fine and handsome in itself but it has nothing to say to the Cathedral'.[22] Holford advocated a less formal scheme, only part of which was built, with architecture designed by Trehearne and Norman, later becoming notorious as 'Paternoster Square'. Richardson's sketches remain as 'masterly' as Holford described them, in a tight roll in the Bedford Record Office, but it remains an open question whether Summerson's criticisms and Holford's suspicions that the reality would be less delightful were justified.

figure 91
Lamp post, Park Crescent, London

As well as such large scale campaigns, Richardson was frequently in the papers in the 1950s over apparently small matters such as the installation of a concrete lamp standard outside Avenue House. These caught the imagination of a public tired of bureaucracy, sameness and low-quality in the design of public amenities. Richardson's interest in street furniture, as in almost all other matters, went back early in his career, and one of his 'Architectural Causerie' columns in the *Architects' Journal* in 1919 was on the subject of lamp posts. He designed cast iron lamp posts with fluted columns and narrow tubular lanterns for the City of Cambridge in the 1950s, and a smaller version of the same design for Park Crescent in London. His concern for these details, for paving surfaces and good benches, if not always his preferred solution, was similar to the anxieties of the influential 'Townscape' and 'Outrage' columns of the *Architectural Review*, compiled by Gordon Cullen and Ian Nairn respectively. Like him, they understood William Blake's meaning of doing good in minute particulars, and it is often the small details of Richardson's buildings that contribute charm to otherwise inexpressive compositions.

'PROGRESS' A SATIRE – RICHARDSON AND MODERNISM

In 1931, Richardson published, as one of a series of fantasy drawings in the *Builder* magazine, '"Progress" A Satire'. The meaning is self-explanatory. On the left, Modernity approaches, with a dense city, tall buildings, motor roads and hoardings. Some of the country dwellers on the right of the picture have taken to the trees, like road protesters on the Newbury By-pass, even though the trees themselves are being cut down, while avenging deities (based on Scylla and the Harpies in John Flaxman's illustrations to the *Odyssey*) loom in the sky. The period around 1930 marked a turning point not only for English architects, but for almost every thinking person, when the forces of industrialism seemed more than ever dominating and malign. The sense of loss and call for defensive action is apparent in Clough Williams-Ellis's tract *England and the Octopus*, in 1928. Thomas Sharp's *Town and Countryside*, 1932, opened with a photograph, a real-life version of Richardson's painting, in which a woman and child at the edge of an idyllic wood lead the eye to a background of encroaching houses. His final chapter, 'Is there any hope?' has difficulty in answering in the affirmative. The criticisms of the existing order are similar to Richardson's: 'Civic expression is being neutralised by country cottage architecture of the same false tradition which debases the countryside.'[23]

Artists responded according to their medium and generation. Ralph Vaughan Williams, eight years older than Richardson, wrote *Job, a Masque for Dancing* in 1930, in which, following William Blake's interpretation of the Biblical story, palpable evil is eventually defeated by faith and hope. Benjamin Britten's cantata *Our Hunting Fathers*, 1936, depicts an increasing alienation of man and nature, with no hope at all. Among architects, the same generational split occurred between those who had known the more hopeful times before 1914 and those of Britten's generation (he was born in 1913), who felt the need for more drastic measures. An equivalent difference of attitude divided architects. Members of Richardson's generation, such as Charles Holden, H.S. Goodhart-Rendel and Robert Atkinson, experimented around 1930 in abolishing historical reference and ornament from their work. Only a younger generation felt that the desperate circumstances needed a complete *tabula rasa*, and found inspiration for it in the work of Walter Gropius and Le Corbusier.

The issue of Richardson's opposition to Modernism can too readily be oversimplified. We have seen how, in 1924, he believed himself to be in the process of discovering what Modern architecture should be. After 1930, he did not suddenly change his mind, but he recognised, as did his mentor W.R. Lethaby before his death in 1931, that there was a danger of acquiring, mainly from European examples of the 1920s, ready-made solutions to complex problems of construction, imagery and meaning in architecture which, if assumed as yet another eclectic style, would prevent a deeper working-out of answers. Richardson was an intuitive thinker rather than a theorist, yet, together with various forms of plain abuse of Modernism (occasionally distasteful in their anti-semitism), he succeeded in articulating one element of the counter-argument to Modernism by questioning its evolutionary basis and asserting that good solutions to architectural problems are available at any time. Opinion in some areas has moved in his direction on this. Pevsner's comment on Richardson & Houfe's Ampthill RDC offices as 'quite unbelievable for their date' itself belongs to a vanished age of certainty about linear progress in architectural style.[24] At the same time, Richardson's blanket condemnation of Modernism caused him to overlook aspects within it potentially more congenial to his own outlook. The ideas represented by W.R. Lethaby about expressing the decency of ordinary life through architecture were, in fact, inherent in the New Towns which Richardson condemned, while the New Brutalists occupied themselves with alternatives to high rise housing and the recovery of regional character in the 1960s. The conditions after the Second World

War led to prefabrication and various forms of lightweight and impermanent construction which became a target for Richardson's condemnation. He did not accept modern architecture's claims to be inherently more 'democratic' than his own manner of work, writing of the Royal Festival Hall in 1951 that, 'no building could have been better designed to bring a sense of inferiority to uncultured citizens.'[25]

During the 1950s many academicians, Sir Edward Maufe, Vincent Harris, Hubert Worthington and others, who, like Richardson, had begun practice before 1914, received large-scale commissions, so that by the end of the decade there was more potential for a 'Battle of the Styles' than there had been in the 1930s. Rather than any structural change in the architectural profession, however, the

figure 92
'Progress' A Satire, 1931

old establishment gave way to a new one, so that Modernism exacerbated the underlying problems of making architecture more responsive to the needs of ordinary people when it had intended to solve them.

It is clear, from 'Progress' A Satire, as from other sources, that Richardson was concerned with the criticism of a whole tendency in civilisation which he felt was endangering mankind. He was not alone in this, but it seems necessary to rescue him from being described either as a nostalgist or as a rigid architectural stylist by emphasising his place in a sequence of radical critics of industrialism from Carlyle, Emerson, Ruskin and Samuel Butler onwards, authors he himself read in early life. Richardson was one of the few academic architects of his time to consider the political meaning of his work, in a body of writing which has remained less well known: his essay 'Erewhon come True' in 1936, for example, referring to Samuel Butler's satire on the nineteenth century in the form of a world where machines are forbidden. The belief that everything went wrong around 1830 was shared by Modernists, though Richardson continued to demonstrate a discriminating appreciation of Victorian architecture. Like Sir Stephen Tallents, his patron at the Empire Marketing Board, Richardson could see in his own time a shift from the expansion achieved through industry and imperialism, towards what he hoped would be a form of post-industrial society. In architecture, he liked to proclaim the unique nature of Englishness, and saw this as the product of social and political evolution which still had meaning as a pattern for the future. His prescription in 1936 was for a resettlement of the country with small farms, an answer which unites the Tory and the Anarchist. Like Ferdinand Tonnies, Richardson saw the problems of industrialism as arising partly from a lack of self-

regulating scale. This sense of appropriate size, a natural way of thinking for an architect, was transferred in his mind to social issues as well. In one of his two radio interviews with John Betjeman in 1956, Richardson defended his attachment to the eighteenth century, saying 'there's no freakish whim in my adoration of the eighteenth century, I use it as a measuring scale. It's enabled me to measure backwards and forwards.' He also frequently invoked William Morris in terms of the need to connect with a more fundamental reality through the sensuous experience of objects. After 1930, Richardson's increasing concern with the survival of craftsmanship was his personal contribution to realising his social vision through his professional work. Again, he was not alone, but even in our present far from satisfactory state of craft skills, it is difficult to understand how close to total collapse craftsmanship was in the years after the Second World War.

There are still further aspects of Richardson's thinking to be explored. In a civilisation under siege, he reacted in a similar way to the German critic and essayist Walter Benjamin (1892–1940), who began to compose his unfinished book on the *Passages* or covered shopping arcades of Paris in 1930. Benjamin, the saturnine Marxist intellectual, now world-famous although almost unrecognised in his lifetime, and Richardson the conservative academician may not appear to have much in common, apart from overlapping life spans, but the interpretation of Benjamin's arcades project offered by Susan Buck-Morss in *The Dialectics of Seeing* provides an unexpected angle on Richardson's relationship to a deeper cultural strand of Modernism than that expressed in buildings of concrete and steel. The period between the Battle of Waterloo and the Revolution of 1848 emerges in both Benjamin and Richardson as deeply significant for the understanding of modernity in all its forms. Richardson even wrote an article about the *'Passages'* of London in 1919. In Benjamin's words, about the 'Angel of History', as in Richardson's illustration, Progress is a storm, and the historian looks backward at the destruction of 'material nature'. Richardson's writings, particularly his book on *Georgian England*, are a montage of documentary information, allowed to speak for itself and deliberately not interpreted according to any grand schema, and thus connected, even if at long distance, to what Buck-Morss describes as 'the principle of montage as a *constructive* principle'.[26] Benjamin, like Richardson, was deeply ambivalent about 'progress' but at the same time imaginatively stimulated by its manifestations.

The analogy between Richardson and Benjamin must allow for the even greater differences between them, but it may at least suggest that to understand Richardson properly we need not accept his life's work only at its face value, or view it as diminished by elements of inconsistency, but may also use our imagination to construct from it our own solutions to the still-present problems of modernity.

oppposite · figure 93
Sir Albert Richardson at Avenue House, photographed by Michael Wickham for *House & Garden*, 1957

Chronology

1880	Born at 33D Middleton Road, Hackney, eldest of three children of Albert Edmund Richardson, printer, and his wife Mary Ann, daughter of Thomas Richardson of Highgate (not related). Educated at Boys' British School, Highgate
1895	Articled to Victor Page, architect, Gray's Inn Road
1898	Assistant to Evelyn Hellicar, 11 Serjant's Inn and attended evening classes at Birkbeck College on building construction and freehand drawing, also employed as a student teacher of architectural history
1902	Assistant to Leonard Stokes, Great Smith Street, Westminster
1903	Assistant to Frank T. Verity, 7 Sackville Street, Piccadilly. Married Elizabeth Byers
1906	Lectureship at Regent Street Polytechnic, and set up practice in Red Lion Street, soon joined in partnership by C. Lovett Gill
1909	Birth of Kathleen Richardson, only child. Move to Cavendish House, St Albans. Richardson & Gill offices at 46 Great Russell Street
1913	Delivered Carpenters Company Lectures at University College. Richardson & Gill offices at 41 Russell Square
1914	Publication of *Monumental Classic Architecture in Great Britain and Ireland*
1916–18	Served as Lieutenant in Royal Flying Corps, working at School of Military Aeronautics at Reading, also at Farnborough and Salvage Section, Southampton
1919	Appointed Professor of Architecture, University College, London (Bartlett School). Appointed editor, *Architects' Journal*. Moved to Avenue House, Ampthill
1932	Award of RIBA Bronze Medal for London Architecture to St Margaret's House, Wells Street
1936	Elected ARA
1939	Termination of partnership with C. Lovett Gill, elected member of Royal Fine Art Commission (served until 1956), marriage of Kathleen Richardson to E.A.S. Houfe
1939–45	Transfer of Bartlett School to Cambridge, rooms in St Catherine's College
1943	Master of the Art Workers Guild
1944	Elected full RA
1945	Partnership with E.A.S. Houfe, offices at 31 Old Burlington Street and at Avenue House, Ampthill; S.P.A. Holland and R.F. Britain became partners in 1959
1947	Retirement from Bartlett School. Opening of Royal Academy School of Architecture. Royal Gold Medal for Architecture
1952	Richardson & Houfe offices in Queen Anne Street
1954	Elected President of Royal Academy (served two terms until 1958)
1956	Appointed KCVO
1957	BBC television programme: 'At Home, Sir Albert Richardson'. Battle over Ampthill lamp posts
1958	Death of Lady Richardson
1964	3 February, death of Sir Albert Richardson at Avenue House

List of Works

This is a first attempt at a list of works by Sir Albert Richardson and published illustrations of them. It is based on a variety of sources, including journals, volumes of The Buildings of England and Ireland, Richardson's early account books (kindly communicated by Simon Houfe) and photograph albums. It is not comprehensive. Works from 1908 to 1939 were undertaken by the partnership of Richardson & Gill and no attempt has been made to give separate attributions to the partners. From 1945, Richardson was in practice with his son-in-law, Eric Houfe, as Richardson & Houfe, later Richardson, Houfe & Partners. Some buildings are separately attributed to Houfe, following indications by Simon Houfe.

Information on demolitions and the execution or non-execution of works presented here is fragmentary. Works are included under the year of commission, where known, otherwise according to date of first publication of designs.

Richardson claimed to have played a part, to differing degrees, in the design of the following buildings by Frank T. Verity: Scala Theatre, Charlotte Street (demolished); Flats in Portland Place; Flats in Cleveland Row; Regent Street frontages between Burlington Street and Conduit Street and Regent Street Polytechnic.

1906

- Architectural Treatment for Waterloo Place (exh. RA 1907)

1910

- Euston Station, suggestion for its reconstruction.
  Town Planning Review, I, 1910, p.263
- Glamorgan County Offices, Cardiff (competition design jointly with S.D. Adshead)

1911

- His Majesty's Theatre (later New Theatre, now Opera House), Quay Street, Manchester (with Horace Farquharson)
  Architectural Review, XXXI, November 1911, pp.278–82; *Architects' & Builders' Journal*, XXXIV, pp.662, 673; XXXV, pp.560–3; XXXVI, pp.240, 258–9; XXXVII, pp.366, 371, 375, 377, 380

1912

- Regent Street Quadrant, competition design for *Builder* magazine
  Builder, CIII, 12 July, 1912, plate; CVI, 1914, p.101–2 (revised design for Swan & Edgar); *Town Planning Review*, III, July 1912, p.154
- Scheme for embodying the facade of the Old General Post Office (by Sir Robert Smirke) in a design for a National Gallery for Sculpture
  Architects' & Builders' Journal, XXXVI, p.221
- Wrought iron gates to doorway of a house near Cambridge
  Architects' & Builders' Journal, XXXVI, p.586
- Thomas Cranmer Memorial, Jesus College Chapel, Cambridge (sculptor A.B. Joy)
  Architects' & Builders' Journal, XXXVIII, 1913, p.162

1913

- House at Khartoum, Egypt
  Architects' & Builders' Journal, XXXVII, p.65
- The Clint, Dawlish [E.H. Weekenfield]
- La Quinta, Dawlish [Major J.W. Salmon]
- Blagdon & Westmeath Memorials, Honiton [Miss E. Blagdon Garden]
- 72–74 Jermyn Street [Mr E. Marinmer]
- Tor Royal Cottages, Bradninch Manor, Princetown [Duchy of Cornwall]
- Stoke Climsland Parish Room [Duchy of Cornwall]
  Architects' Journal, XLIX, 28 May, 1919, p.377
- The Manor Farm House, Whiteford, Stoke Climsland
  Builder, CIX, 1915, p.104–5; *Architects' Journal*, XLIX, 28 May, 1919, p.376
- Pipingford Park, Agent's House, Cottages (alterations) [Capt Banbury]
- Hotel, Baker Street/Dorset Street [Wimperis]
- Imperial (Duchy) Hotel, Princetown [Duchy of Cornwall]
- Ashley Memorial, Romsey Abbey, Hants (sculptor Emile Fuchs)
  Architects' & Builders' Journal, XXXVII, pl. 29 October; *Builder*, CV, 1913, p.478; CIX, 1919, p.154; illustrated in Lawrence Weaver, *Memorials and Monuments*, 1915
- Southampton House, Nos.43–46 Southampton Buildings, Holborn
  Architects' & Builders' Journal, XXXVII, 18 May, 1913, p.571

- Mayfair Hotel, 19 Berkeley Street, Piccadilly
  Architects' & Builders' Journal, XXXVII, 11 June, 1913, pp.615, 617

1914

- Proposal for completion of Somerset House
  Builder, CVI, 1914, p.15
- St Paul's Bridge (competition)
  Builder, CVI, 1914, p.175
- Cottages, Fordington, Dorchester (reworking of plans submitted by local architect) [Duchy of Cornwall]
- Princetown Cottages [Duchy of Cornwall]
  Builder, CIX, 1915, p.103
- Cottages, Bucklawren [Duchy of Cornwall]
- 32 Queen Anne's Gate (staircase) [Lady Allendale]
- Moorgate Hall, 73–93 Finsbury Pavement, EC [Herbert Reeves/ London & North Estate Co.] demolished
  Architects' & Builders' Journal, XXXIX, 1914, pl. 27 May; *Architectural Review*, XXXIX, 1916, pp.138–9; *Builder*, CVI, pl. Jan 2; CXI, 1916, p.294 (including frontage for London, County and Westminster Bank)
- Royal Theatre, Torquay (with F.G. Moore, architect, Torquay) Winner of limited competition. Not executed
  Architects' & Builders' Journal, XL, pl. 19 August; *Builder* CVII, 28 August 1914, p.216 & plate, p.217; CXII, 1917, pp.146, 150–1
- New Office, Liskeard [Duchy of Cornwall]
  Builder, CIX, 1915, p.102
- No.8 Victoria Square, SW [Ralph C. Leach & Co.]
- 10 Berkeley Street, W1 [London & North Estate Co.]
  Architects' & Builders' Journal, XLII, 1915, pl. 28 July; *Builder*, CIX, 1915, p.272
- 27–29 Tothill Street, London SW1 [Technical Journals Ltd.]
  Architects' & Builders' Journal, XLI, pl. 5 May
- Garage at St Albans
  Architects' & Builders' Journal, XLI, 1915, pl. 19 August
- Farmhouses, Postbridge [Duchy of Cornwall]
  Architects' & Builders' Journal, XLV, 1917, pl. 10 January; *Architects' Journal*, XLIX, 28 May, 1919, p.374–5
- Two Bridges Hotel, Dartmoor [Duchy of Cornwall]
- Marsh Farm, Landulph, Gurnet Court, West Harptree (alterations), Cottages, Frenchbere [Duchy of Cornwall]
- Hilltop, Sunningdale (design work begun 1913, contract signed 23 February 1914) [Sir Bruce Ha, KCB]
  Architects' & Builders' Journal, XL, 1914, pl. 23 September; *Builder* CVI, 1914, 24 April, pp.498, 500, 501; *Architectural Review*, XLV, 1919, pp.18–21; Lawrence Weaver, *Small Country Houses of To-Day*, Vol.2, London, Country Life, 1919, pp.184–8
- The Mansion, Leatherhead [Herbert Reeves]
- St Paul's Bridge (competition design)
  Builder, CVI, 1914, p.756; *Architectural Review*, XXXVII, 1915, p.15

1915

- Vancouver pedestal [Bruce Joy]
- Bronze Gates [Messrs. Spetal & Clarke, Frome, for West Harptree]
- Farm at St Judy, Bothwigan [Duchy of Cornwall]
- Lodge at Chagford [Duchy of Cornwall]
- Vicarage, Princetown [Duchy of Cornwall]

figure 94
Memorial to Maud Ashley, Romsey Abbey, 1913 (sculptor Emil Fuchs)

figure 95
Hilltop, Sunningdale, 1919

- Cottage, Whiteford [Duchy of Cornwall]
- Ascot Church, Altar Rails [Sir C. Ryan]
- Second pair of cottages, Stoke Climsland [Duchy of Cornwall]
- Silver-Gilt cup presented to Gonville & Caius College, Cambridge, by General Sir Bruce Meade Hamilton, GCB, KCVO, and Officers of the General Staff, First Army, Central Force, in Memory of 1915
  Architects' & Builders' Journal, XLI, 1915, pl. 27 October

1916

- St Michael's Church, Princetown (alterations) [Duchy of Cornwall]
- 9–11 Fulwood Place, WC2 [Herbert Reeves]
- St Matthew's, Bayswater [alterations]
- Farm at Bellever [Duchy of Cornwall]
  Architects' Journal, XLII, 28 May, 1919, p.374, 378
- Cottage, Hexworthy [Duchy of Cornwall]

1917

- 124 Harley Street (alterations) [Major McAdam Eccles]
- Cottages at Fordington [Duchy of Cornwall]
  Architects' & Builders' Journal, XLV, 1917, pl. 9 May
- Bungalow at Huccaby [Duchy of Cornwall]
  Architects' Journal, XLII, 28 May, 1919, p.374
- Church Tower, Bradninch [Duchy of Cornwall]
- Project for London Fire Insurance Office
  Builder CXII, pp.224–5; *Architects' Journal*, XLI, 21 May, 1919

1919

- Proposed villages at Kit Hill and Hingston [Duchy of Cornwall]
- 43–52 Moorgate Street [Herbert Reeves]
  Builder, CXIII, 1917, p.112; *Architectural Review*, LIX, 1921, pp.5–10

1920

- Offices over St James's Park Station [R.E. Knapp]
- The Hale, Wendover [Sir Bruce Hamilton] (enlargement and alteration of C17 house)
- Extension to No.33 Brompton Square [D. Erskine]
- 50–55 Moorgate Street (conversion) [Herbert Reeves]
- Blue Hayes, Broad Clyst, Exeter, Devon (alterations) [Capt. Imbert-Terry]
  Architects' Journal, XLIII, 23 June, 1920, p.783
- Nos.62–65 Leadenhall Street, EC (Richardson & Gill with A.H. Kersey, architect) [Messrs Mcfachearn]
  Builder CXXII, 1922, pp.936–7, 942–3; *Architects' Journal*, LII, 1920, p.436
- Arundel Hotel
- Warbrook, Eversley, Hants (alterations) [W. Ranken]
- Eartham Village Hall, W. Sussex [Sir William Bird]
- Homelands Farm, Ampthill [Mrs Ridgeway]

1921

- Clophill Church, Bedfordshire
- Marden Hall, Herts. (alterations) [Major C.E. Banbury]

figure 96
Concrete cottages, Scilly Isles

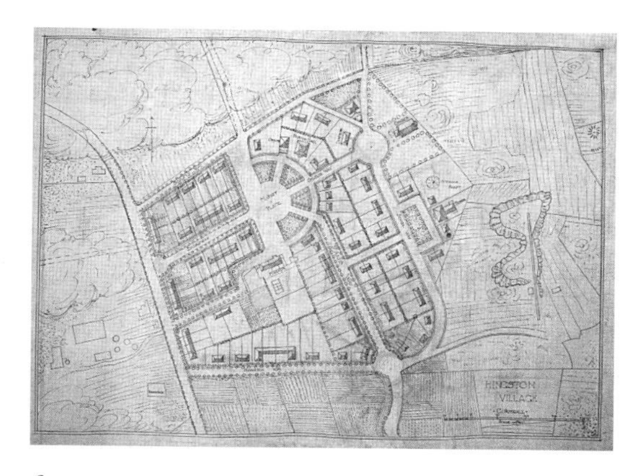

figure 97
Plan of proposed village, Hingston, for Duchy of Cornwall, *c.*1920

- Alameda Gates, Ampthill [Ampthill UDC]
- 45–53 Moorgate Street [Dr Rabinovitch] Demolished
  Builder, CXXIV, 1923, pp.17, 889–90
- Thorp Monument, Ardbreknish, Argyll [Mrs Thorp]
- Proposed house, Denham [H.R. Davies]
- 30 & 32 Queen Anne's Gate [Lady Allendale]
- Cottages at St Mary's, Scilly [Duchy of Cornwall]

1922

- Anatomy Building (Gower Street), University College, London
- No 37 Soho Square (alterations) [Messrs. Love Sons]
  Builder, CXXIII, pp.653, 660, 663–5
- Mitre Hotel, Oxford [Mitre Hotel Ltd.]
  Builder, CXXV, 1923, pp.712–3, 715, 717, 720, 727, 777
- Church Tower, Princetown [Duchy of Cornwall]
- Lydford Castle
- Goldings, Essex [Lord Stanmore]
  Builder, CXXVIII, 1925, pp.378, 380
- Combe Down, Shawford, Hants [H.R. Love]
- Forest Inn, Hexworthy [Duchy of Cornwall]
- King's Head, Ampthill [Bedfordshire Territorials]
  Builder, CXXIV, 1923, p.82
- Little Paddocks, Sunninghill [Col. Horlick]
  Builder, CXXVIII, 1925, p.445 (panel in gunroom door, carved by P.G. Bentham); CXXIX, 1925, p.461

1923

- Completion of upper floor of 1891 Chadwick Wing, University College, London
- York House 56–60 Moorgate [Messrs. Reeves]
  Builder, CXXIV, 1923, p.888
- Main Street, Hughtown, Isles of Scilly [Duchy of Cornwall]
  Builder, CXXIII, 1922, p.234
- 'Archerton', Postbridge, Devon [Lady Bennett]
  Builder, CXXV, 1923, p.482
- 43 Regent Square
- 'Clonboy', Englefield Green, Surrey [Lady de Vesci]
- Cottages at Porthloo [Duchy of Cornwall]
  Builder, CXXII, 1922, p.237
- 'Reydon', Walton-on-Thames (alterations) [B.G. White]
- Darwin Building, Gower Street, University College, London
  Builder, CXXIV, p.770 (RA exhibition), built in much simplified form, 1959–64
- Prince Hall, Dartmoor (project for sporting hotel)
  Builder, CXXV, 1923, p.484
- Proposal for the reconstruction of Temple Bar
  Builder, CXXIV, 1923, p.880
- Memorial to Thomas Weelkes, St Bride's Church, Fleet Street (modelled by P.G. Bentham)

1924

- Parsons Cottage, Postbridge [Commander Lapage]
- Dennis Farm, Reterth [Duchy of Cornwall]
  Builder, CXXVI, 1924, p.580
- Bungalow at Brownberry, Cornwall [Duchy of Cornwall]
  Builder, CXXVI, 1924, p.587
- Warbrook, Hants [Sir John Stirling-Maxwell of Pollok, Bt.]
- Stoke Hampton [Duchy of Cornwall]
- 47 Pembroke Square (alterations) [Cecil J. Norbury]
- Avonmouth house (alterations) [Admiral E. Reeves]
- Shop & Cottages, St Mary's, Scilly [Duchy of Cornwall]
- Edencliffe, Holcombe [Edward Crewe]
- Fenchurch Buildings, 9–13 Fenchurch Street [Reeves & Co.]
- 65 Fenchurch Street, by F. Taperell & Haase, 1924–27, based on designs by Richardson & Gill

figure 98
Rebuilding of High Street, Hugh Town, Scilly Isles, *c.*1922

1925

- Leith House, Gresham Street and Wood Street [Reeves & Co.] Consultant engineer Sven Bylander
  Builder, CXXVI, 1924, p.54 (perspective by J.D.M. Harvey, exhibited at Royal Academy); CXXX, 1926, pp.266, 278, 280–2; *Architectural Review*, LXIX, June, p.137 (detail of carving); LXX, July 1926, pp.18–19
- Design for British Pavilion, Paris International Exhibition,
  Builder CXXVIII, 1925, p.830

1927

- Emlyn House, Leatherhead, Surrey (addition of loggia)
  Architects' Journal, 12 Oct 1927, pp.463–4
- Stand at Holland Park Ice Rink [Empire Marketing Board]
  Builder, CXXXII, 1927, p.766
- Stone House, 136 Bishopsgate
  Builder, CXXXII, 1927, p.612; *Architect & Building News*, CXIX, 1928, p.783; *Builder*, CXXXIV, 1928, pp.674, 677
- Altar and Reredos, St Bride's Church, Fleet Street
  Builder, CXXXIII, 1927, p.930
- Memorial Hall (Convocation Hall), University College, London (conversion of All Saints, Gordon Square)
  Builder, CXXXIII, 1927, p.10–12; *Architects' Journal*, LXV, 29 June, 1927, pp.929–36
- Town Hall, Dulverton, Somerset [commissioned by Mrs Herbert]
  Builder, CXXXIII, 1927, pp.766–7, 771–2

1928

- Empire Pavilion, Canadian Exhibition, Toronto
  Builder, CXXXV, 1928, pp.706, 708–9, 715, 718–20
- Department of Chemistry, University College, London (project)
  Architect & Building News, CXIX, 1928, p.688; *Builder*, CXXXIV, 1928, p.848

1929

- Altar, Harlington Church, Bedfordshire
  Builder, CXXXIVI, 1929, p.942
- Empire Pavilion, North-East Coast Exhibition, Newcastle
  Architect & Building News, CXXI, 1929, p.647; *Builder*, CXXXVI, 1929, p.917
- Princess Elizabeth Hostel, Cromwell House, Highgate
  Builder, CXXXVI, 1929, p.814; CXXXVIII, 1930, pp.475–8
- Oakwood Court Flats, Holland Park
  Builder, CXXXIVII, 1929, p.469; CXXXVIII, 1930, pp.857–60

1930

- Shop front and interior for B.T. Batsford Ltd., 15 North Audley Street, W1
  Architect & Building News, CXXIV, p.783
- Antwerp Exhibition Buildings
  Builder CXXXVIII, 1930, pp.300–1
- Department of Chemical Engineering, University College, London
  Builder CXXXVIII, 1930, p.346
- The House in the Field (now Mulberry Hill), Wendover [Sir Stanley Reed]
  Builder CXXXVIII, 1930, pp.706, 708
- St Margaret's House, 19–23 Wells Street [for Arthur Sanderson & Sons]
  Architects' Journal, LXXIV, 1931, pp.771–2; LXXVI, 1932, pp.32, 689; *Builder*, CXXXIX, 1930, p.101; CXL 1931, pp.194–5, CXLIII 1933, p.89

figure 99
Empire Pavilion, Canadian Exhibition, Toronto, 1928

figure 100
Empire Pavilion, North-East Coast Exhibition, Newcastle, 1929

- Flats (Thackeray Court), Kensington Square
  Builder, CXL 1931, p.843
- Guildford Cathedral (competitions designs)
  Builder, CXL 1931, p.491
- Chevithorne Barn, Devon (remodelling)
- The Lodge, Whipsnade (destroyed by fire 1939)
  'The Architectural Work of Sir Albert Richardson in Bedfordshire, 1919–64', *Bedfordshire Magazine*, XIII, 1972, pp.176–83

1931

- St Christopher, Round Green, Luton (first scheme; completed to different design 1937, chancel added 1959, church hall also by Richardson)
  Builder, CXLI 1931, p.147; CLII, 1937, p.1027
- Monument to R101 Disaster, Cardington, Beds
- Staple Hall, Bishopsgate
- Stone House Court, Bishopsgate
- Foster Court, Malet Place, adaptation of Shoolbred's mattress factory, with clock turret, 1937

1932

- St Mary, Shelton, Bedfordshire (repairs, including new rood beam by Percy Bentham)
  Builder, CXLII 1931, pp.586, 597
- St Mary, Eaton Socon, Huntingdonshire (rebuilding after fire)
  Builder, CXLIII 1932, pp.90–94
- RIBA Headquarters competition design
  Architect & Building News, CXXX, p.196; repr. Margaret Richardson, *66 Portland Place*, London, RIBA Publications Ltd., 1984, p.9

1933

- Esmond Court, Kensington
  Builder, CXLIV 1933, pp.71, 89
- University College, London completion of wings (RA Exhibition)
  Architect & Building News, CXXIV, 1933, p.168; *Builder*, CXLIV 1933, p.775
- Marlon House, 71–74 Mark Lane
  Architects' Journal, LXXX, pp.884–5

1934

- Flats (Endsleigh Court), Upper Woburn Place
  Architect & Building News, CXLI, 1935, pp.111–112; *Architects' Journal*, LXXIX, 1934, p.809; LXXXI, 1935, pp.62–4; *Builder*, CXLVI 1934, p.978
- Gustave Tuck Theatre, University College (within William Wilkins building)
  Architects' Journal, LXXIX, 1934, pp.792–4
- Jockey Club, Newmarket
  Builder, CXLVI 1934, p.798 (model); CXL 1936, p.973 (drawing for single-storey scheme exh.RA); CLII, 1937, pp.100–104 (completed scheme); *Country Life*, LXXV, 1934, pp.482–3
- Bramford Hall, Suffolk, alterations [Sir Percy Loraine]

1935

- Ripon Hall, Oxford, new wing
- Church Hall, Bricket Wood, Herts
- St Stephen's Hall, St Albans, Herts
- Pelmet for Royal Academy

1936

- Royal Pavilion and Royal Stand, Ascot Racecourse (demolished)
  Builder, CL 1936, p.922

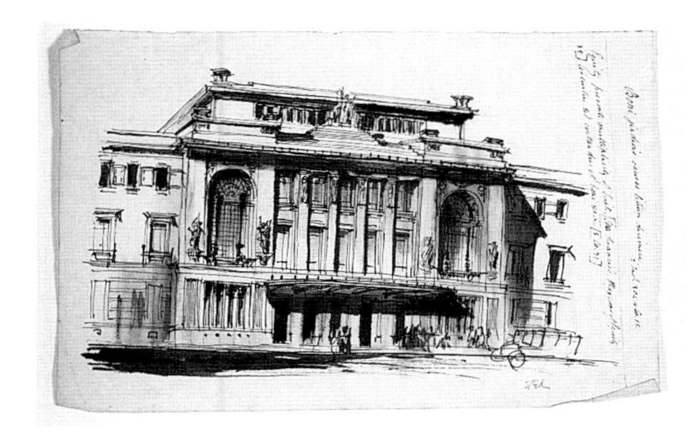

figure 101
Sketch for buildings for University College, London, *c.*1935, drawn on a leaf from an 18th-century copybook

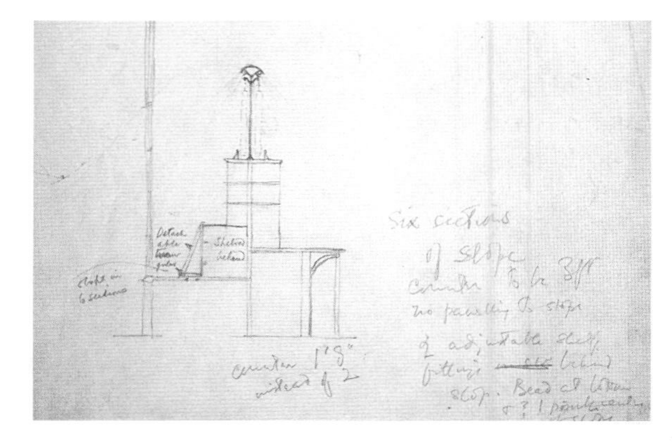

figure 102
B.T. Batsford, 15 North Audley Street, details of window display unit

- Clifton House, Euston Road
  Architect & Building News, CL, 1937, pp.102–3; *Builder*, CL 1936, pp.1220–1221
- The Hall, Grove End Road, St John's Wood, London NW8 (flats)
  Builder CLI, 1936, pp.299, 304
- Flitwick Manor, Beds. Restoration [Colonel Lyall]

1937

- Village Hall, Great Barrington, Gloucestershire [Col. Wingfield]
- St Andrew, Much Hadham, Herts (light fittings)
- Homelands (now Chiltern Hill House), Wendover [Miss Compton]
- St Mary, Wendover, Bucks, Memorial to Sir Bruce Hamilton
- All Saints, Southill, Beds. Font
- Harlington Manor, Beds., new wing [Colonel Tabor]
- Church of the Holy Cross, Greenford, Middlesex (first design 1937, constructed to revised design during war)
  Architects' Journal, XCVI, 1942, pp.25–9; *Architectural Design & Construction*, XII, 1942, pp.38–9; *Builder* CLXII, 1942, pp.27–31

1938

- North London Collegiate School, Canons Park, Edgware (new hall and other additions, 1939–40; Drawing School, 1957)
  Builder CLIV, 1938, p.893
- John White Factory, Lime Street, Rushden, Northants.
  Simon Houfe, 'The Architectural Work of Sir Albert Richardson in Bedfordshire, 1919–64', *Bedfordshire Magazine*, XIII, 1972, pp.176–83
- University College, London. Side gates to Torrington Place
- Woldmere, Millfield Lane, Highgate
- Home Farm, Milton Ernest, Beds., alterations [Col. Starey]
  Simon Houfe, 'The Architectural Work of Sir Albert Richardson in Bedfordshire, 1919–64', *Bedfordshire Magazine*, XIII, 1972, pp.176–83

1939

- Russell Square House, Russell Square
  Builder, CLVI, 1939, p.934
- St Michael, Millbrook, Beds. Reredos and candlesticks

1940

- Chapel, Merchant Taylors School
  Architect & Building News, CLXII, 1940, p.111; *Builder*, CLVIII, 1940, p.561 (RA Exhibition)
- St Paul's Cathedral, memorial to Pilot Officer Fiske (sculptor Richard Garle)
- Shire Hall, Bedford, competition design (not executed)
  Simon Houfe, 'The Architectural Work of Sir Albert Richardson in Bedfordshire, 1919–64', *Bedfordshire Magazine*, XIII, 1972, pp.176–83

1941

- Rebuilding of Abingdon Street
  Builder, CLVIII, 1941, p.455; *Architectural Design and Construction* (RA Exhibition)

1942

- Royal Academy Plan for London (two illustrations),
  Architect & Building News, CLXXII, 1942, pp.77–8;
- School House, Hawnes, Bedford
  Builder, CLXII, 1942, p.405 (RA Exhibition)
- Chillingham Castle, Northumberland, restoration after fire [Lord Tankerville]

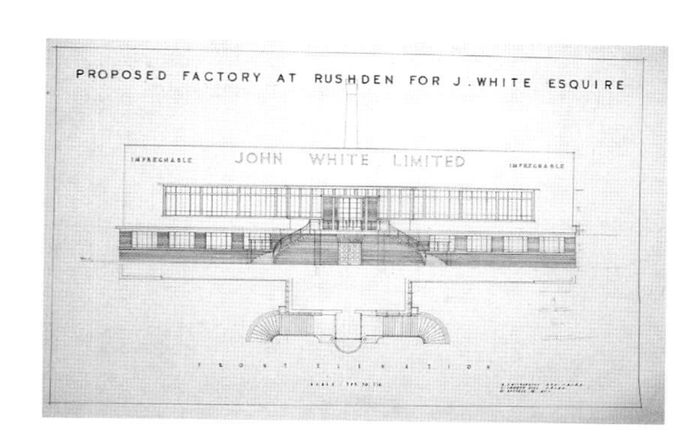

above left · figure 103
North London Collegiate School, Canons Park, Edgware, design for new buildings, 1938

left · figure 104
John White Factory, Rushden, Northants, 1938

above · figure 105
Competition design for Shire Hall, Bedford, model, *c.*1940

1943

- Premises for the Chancery Lane Safe Deposit,
  Builder, CLXIV, p.463, executed 1947–53
- Town Hall, Higham Ferrers, Northamptonshire
  Builder, CLXIV, 1943, p.412

1944

- Cathedral Church of York, new stalls
  Builder, CLXVI, 1944, p.462
- Remodelling of University College, London. Post-war restoration of University College including interiors of Wilkins Building, with Library by T.L. Donaldson.
  Builder, CLXVI, 1944, p.379 (RA Exhibition – scheme for whole site); CLXXII, 1947, p.502 (RA Exhibition – Great Hall); CLXXVI, 1949, p.558 (RA Exhibition – reconstruction of dome)
- St Peter's Church, Harrow, design for reredos

1945

- New Housing Layout, Oliver Street, Ampthill, Beds. (RA Exhibition – model). Built 1949
  Builder, CLXVIII, 1945, p.508
- Wherwell Priory, Hants, restoration after fire [Col. Jenkins]

1946

- The 'Battle of Britain' Memorial, King Henry VII's Chapel, Westminster Abbey (with Hugh Easton, designer of memorial window, A.F. Hardiman, sculptor and J. Seymour Lindsay, silversmith)
  Builder, CLXXIV, 1948, pp.31–5
- Cambridge Botanic Garden, new library and lecture theatre (RA Exhibition)
  Architects' Journal, CIII, 1946, p.417
- Cathedral Church, York: Library (RA Exhibition)
  Builder, CLXX, 1946, p.484
- St Edward, Cambridge (repairs)
- St James's, Piccadilly (repairs, mainly completed 1954, spire completed 1968)
  Builder, CLXX, 1946, pp.474–5; CLXXXI, 1951, pp.441–4
- Laboratories, Exeter
  Builder, CLXX, 1946, p.479
- Cottages at Old Warden, Bedfordshire

1947

- St. Etheldreda, Hatfield, Herts (pulpit and processional cross)
- Tallow Chandlers Hall (repairs, with H. Edmund Matthews)
- Barons Court, Co. Tyrone, remodelling (RA Exhibition)
  Builder, CLXXVI, p.626
- Melford Hall, Long Melford, Suffolk (restoration after fire) [Lady Hyde Parker]
- Viscount Southwood Memorial, St James's Church, Piccadilly, with A.E. Hardiman, sculptor (RA Exhibition model)
  Builder, CLXXII, p.439; CLXXVI, 1949, p.616; CLXXVII, 1949, p.281
- Mausoleum for the Duke of Windsor, Fort Belvedere

1948

- Extensions to Christ's College, Cambridge (RA Exhibition), Chancellor's Building, 1948, Memorial Building, 1950
  Architects' Journal, CXXVII, 1958, p.41; *Builder*, CLXXIV, p.580; CLXXVIII, 1950, pp.549–54

figure 106
Shire Hall, Bedford, sketch

figure 107
Festival of Britain, information kiosk for Corporation of London, 1951, originally sited in St Paul's Garden, moved in 1955

- Door knocker for Ripon Hall, Oxford
  Builder, CLXXIV, p.75
- New Drawing Room, Barnwell Manor, Northants [Duke of Gloucester]

1949

- Building at Trinity Hall, Cambridge
- Reredos, Cross and Candlesticks, Ridley Hall, Cambridge
- Alterations to Gatehouse Building, Trinity Hall, Cambridge
- Trent College, Derby Road, Long Eaton, internal remodelling of chapel
- York Minster, Archbishop Savage Monument, North Choir Aisle, new wooden superstructure
- Westminster Abbey, lectern

1950

- Somerset House, reconstruction of South Wing (RA Exhibition)
  Builder, CLXXVIII, p.589 (RA Exhibition)
- Trinity House, Tower Hill. Reconstruction of bomb-damaged building by Samuel Wyatt, 1793–6, with addition of wing containing Library and Pepys Room, and office building (Woodruff House) to rear (demolished 1990)
  Designed 1950, construction 1952–4
  Builder, CLXXVIII, p.680 (RA Exhibition); CLXXXVI, 1954, pp.712–8; *Country Life*, CXIV, 1953, pp.1288–91
- St Hilda's College, Oxford, (RA Exhibition, 1950); Principal's Lodging completed 1954
  Architects' Journal, CXXXVI, 1957, p.58; *Builder*, CLXXIX, p.61; CC, 1961, p.593
- Council Housing, Barnadiston, Wickhambrook & Hundon, Suffolk

1951

- St Paul's Garden and Information Centre, at corner of New Change and Cannon Street [City of London] (Information Centre resited 1955 at corner of St Paul's Churchyard and Dean's Court. *Buildings of England* wrongly attributes authorship to the City Corporation)
  Architect & Building News, CL, p.178; *Builder*, CLXXX, pp.322, 850–2
- New Technical College, Bedford (RA Exhibition). Not executed
  Builder, CLXXX, p.657
- Coventry Cathedral, competition designs (commended)
  Louise Campbell, *Coventry Cathedral, Art and Architecture in Post War Britain*, Oxford, Clarendon Press, 1996, p.53
- York Minster, Gospel Ambo
- Queens' College, Cambridge, conversion of old chapel into War Memorial Library
- Trinity College, Cambridge, War Memorial in Ante-chapel
- Old People's Bungalows, Higham Ferrers, Northants
  Builder, CLXXXI, 1951, pp.752–4
- Tiranti Shop Front, 72 Charlotte Street, W1
  Builder, CLXXXI, 1951, p.342

1952

- Holy Trinity, Bottisham, Cambridgeshire, west screens
- Bank of England. Reinstatement of original central fireplace in Court Room
- Mornington, Digswell, Herts. Additions [D. Carnegie] (Design by E.A.S. Houfe)

figure 108
Housing, Blackheath Park, 1952

figure 109
St Hilda's College, Oxford, Principal's Lodging, 1954

- St Alfege, Greenwich (restoration after bomb damage of church by Nicholas Hawksmoor, 1711–14)
  Builder, CLXXXII, 1952, pp.401–5
- Housing, Blackheath Park (for London Borough of Greenwich)
  Builder, CLXXXII, 1952, p.741 (RA Exhibition)
- Lawrence Chubb Memorial, Hampstead Heath
  Builder, CLXXXIII, p.390
- Petrol Station for Mobil at Woburn, Beds.

1953

- Desk for Sir Winston Churchill, Chartwell, Kent

1954

- Housing, Fulthorpe Road, Lewisham (for London Borough of Greenwich)
- Woburn Abbey, Beds., elevations for completion of demolished wings
  Builder, CLXXXVI, p.799 (RA Exhibition); CLXXXVII, p.972
- University College, London, Physics Wing
  Builder, CLXXXVI, pp.1106–9
- House in Bromham Road, Bedford [James White]
  Country Life, CXVIII, 1955, pp.856–7; H. Dalton Clifford, *New Houses for Moderate Means*, London, Country Life Ltd., 1957, pp.108–10
- Bracken House, Cannon Street, London [*Financial Times*]
  Architects' Journal, CCV, 1954, p.742; Builder, CLXXXVI, 1954, p.799 (RA Exhibition)

1955

- St Mary, Richmond-on-Thames (remodelling of sanctuary)
- York Minster, Astronomical Clock (with H.J. Stammers, frieze by Frank Dobson)
- St Mary, Cardington, Beds., lectern (carved by Frank Dobson)
- Sir Malcolm Stewart Homes and Common Room, Stewartby, Beds.
  Builder, CXC, p.305
- North London Collegiate School Swimming Bath
- Picture Gallery, Anglesey Abbey, Cambridgeshire [Lord Fairhaven]
- Proposed semi-standard type church for the new towns
  Architecture & Building, XXX, 1955, p.190

1956

- Merchant Taylors Hall (rebuilding after bomb damage)
  Builder, CXCI, p.281 (RA Exhibition)
- Senate House, University of Cambridge (internal restoration, completed 1958)
- Kelmarsh Hall, Northampton (removal of C19 additions to house by James Gibbs)
- Associated Electrical Industries, Grosvenor Place, SW1 (consultant to Wimperis, Simpson & Fyffe)
- House at Weston Patrick, Hants
  Country Life, CXXVIII, 1960, 13 October, pp.816–8

1957

- Sedbergh School, West Yorkshire War Memorial Library in building of 1716
  Country Life, CXXIV, 1958, 10 July, pp.80–1

figure 110
York Minster Astronomical Clock, 1955

figure 111
House in Bromham Road, Bedford, 1954

figure 112
Bryanston Square flats, 1963

1958

- Ripon Cathedral, repair of Chapter House
- Little Coles, Amersham, Bucks
- No.1 Norfolk Road, London NW8
- Pertenhall, Beds. New 'Gun Room' (design by E.A.S. Houfe)

1959

- Westoning Manor, Beds. Garden, conservatory (design by E.A.S. Houfe)
- Tor Mor Distillery and village, Speyside
- Lodge at Woodberry Hall, Beds.

1960

- Stud Farm, Westoning Manor, Beds. (design by E.A.S. Houfe)
- St Hilda's College, Wolfson Building, octagonal lodge, bow to river
- Kenwick Hall, Lincolnshire [Capt. Oscar Dixon] (design by E.A.S. Houfe)
- College of St Mary, Strawberry Hill, new chapel and student residences, including restoration of Horace Walpole's house
  Builder, CXCVIII, 1960, p.872 (RA Exhibition); CCVI, 1964, pp.325–8
- Garden House for General Norman, West Farleigh, Maidstone, Kent

1961

- Round Oak, Windsor
- Stable Block, Ascot for Baron Schroeder

1963

- Stone's Chop House (Clareville House), Panton Street, W1
- Assembly Rooms, Bath (restoration after war damage)
- St Martin, Knebworth (completion of church by Sir Edwin Lutyens)
- Ampthill Rural District Council Offices, Ampthill, Beds
- Bryanston Square flats
  Architects' Journal, CXXI, 1960, p.155
- Seymour Place flats
- Merryfield, Sussex [Ribton Crampton] (design by E.A.S. Houfe)

1965

- St John the Evangelist, Escomb, Co. Durham (restoration)

figure 113
Ampthill RDC Offices, 1963–4

figure 114
Ampthill RDC Offices, drawing by Richardson for cupola, 1963

List of Writings by Sir Albert Richardson

- This list of books and articles is not fully comprehensive. It is based on a bibliography compiled by Simon Houfe with additional material. A number of unsigned pieces are attributed to Richardson on the basis of their presence in his scrapbooks.

1908

- 'Christ's Hospital', contribution to *London Passed and Passing* by Hanslip Fletcher, 1908, pp.63–8
- 'Some Recent "Mansion Flats" in London, Frank T. Verity, architect', *Architectural Review*, XXIII, May, pp.286–95

1910

- 'A Minor City Church', St Benet's, St Paul's Wharf, *Architectural Review*, XXVIII, October, pp.182–88

1911

- *London Houses from 1660 to 1820, A Consideration of their Architecture and Detail*, A.E. Richardson and C. Lovett Gill. B.T. Batsford
- 'Classic Architecture in England and America', *Architects' & Builder's Journal*, XXXIII, January 25, pp.100–01
- 'The Style Neo-Grec', *Architectural Review*, XXX, July, p.25–29
- 'Town Planning, formal or Irregular' (contribution to discussion), *Architect & Builder's Journal*, XXXIV, October 25, p.436
- 'Dublin: An impression' (signed AER), *Architectural Review*, XXXI, October, p.189
- 'The Empire Style in England', I, *Architectural Review*, XXXI, November, p.255–63; II, December, p.315–25
- 'American Buildings' (Paper read before AA Camera Sketch and Debate Club)
- *British Architect* LXXV, p.184

1912

- 'Regent Street. The Brightest Mart in London' (unsigned), *Daily Telegraph*, 28 May, p.6
- 'The New Regent Street Quadrant As It Might Be' (unsigned), *Daily Telegraph*, 1 June, p.18
- 'The Academic in Architecture', RIBA *Journal*, XIX, 31 August, p.683
- 'Architecture from the Classic Standpoint' *Architectural Review*, XXXIII, September, pp.170–72 (signed 'X')
- 'Karl Friedrich Schinkel' *Architectural Review*, XXXIII, February, pp.61–79
- 'London's Bridges, Notable Features of Their Construction', *Evening Standard*, (date missing) p.5
- 'The Restorations of Canina' *Architects' & Builders' Journal*, XXXVI, 20 November, pp.539–43

1913

- 'The Demolition of Southwark Bridge', *Architects' & Builders' Journal*, XXXVII, 26 February, pp.217–8
- 'Tradition in English Architecture' (AER), *Architects' & Builders' Journal*, XXXVII, pp.163–4
- 'The Shop Front of Yesterday', *Architects' & Builders' Journal*, XXXVII, 12 March, p.267 (Scrapbook)
- 'The Hinterland of Euston' (signed 'R'), *Architects' & Builders' Journal*, XXXVIII, 3 September, pp.230–2
- Letter to the *British Architect*, LXXX, signed 'Mentor', 5 September, pp.163–5
- 'Streets of Misadventure', *Architects' & Builders' Journal*, XXXVIII, 10 September, pp.253–4 (editorial, Scrapbook)
- 'Mecklenburgh Square', *Architects' & Builders' Journal*, XXXVIII, 8 October, pp.350–1
- 'Laurentium: The Winter Villa of C. Plinius Caeciulius Secundus', *Architects' & Builders' Journal*, XXXVIII, 22 October, pp.388–90
- Reports of Carpenters Company Lectures at University College, London, 'The Work of English Architects of the Eighteenth Century and Neo-Classic School', *Architects' & Builders' Journal*, LXXXIX, 1913, pp.415; 450; 468–9; 487–8; 520–1; 558–60; 574–5; XL, 1914, pp.10–12; 28–30.
- 'Home for London University – Somerset House', *Daily Telegraph*, 28 Nov, p.14
- 'The Palais de Justice, Paris and its remodelling by Joseph Louis Duc', *Architectural Review*, XXXIV, November, pp.93–4

1914

- *Monumental Classic Architecture in Great Britain and Ireland during the Eighteenth and Nineteenth Centuries*, B.T. Batsford, published 23 April
- [Reviews: *Architect and Builders' Journal* XL, 6 May, p.316–8; *Architectural Record*, New York ('Notable Recent English Books by Richard Franz Bach), pp.475–8; *Athenaeum*, 16 May; *Building News*, 24 April, p.566; *Daily Telegraph*, 1 May, 1914; *Manchester Guardian*, 25 June; *Morning Post; Scotsman* 14 May; *Times Literary Supplement*, 4 June, p.267]
- 'The Palais de Justice, Paris and its remodelling by Joseph Louis Duc' *Architectural Review*, XXXV, January, pp.7–10
- 'Plans for Somerset House', *Field*, 17 January
- 'The Classic Tradition in America', *Architect & Builders' Journal*, XL, 21 January, pp.47–8
- 'Exhibition of Prix de Rome Drawings at the Canada Gallery, Imperial Institute', *Architects' & Builders' Journal*, XL, 25 February, pp.42–3
- 'The Railway Stations of London' (AER), *Architects' & Builders' Journal* XL, 4 March, pp.148–9

- 'King's Cross Improvement Competition' (unsigned), *Architects' & Builders' Journal*, XL, 11 March, 170–172
- 'Nineteenth Century Architecture at Dover', *Builder*, CVI, 12 June, pp.693–4
- 'The Prix de Rome Prize Designs in Architecture', *Builder*, CVII, 15 July, pp.61–5
- 'Jean Charles Krafft, Architecte-Dessinateur', *Architectural Review*, XXXVI, September, pp.52–58
- 'Jacques Ignace Hittorff', *Architectural Review*, XXXVI, December, pp.102–110

1915

- 'Review of the London County Council Survey, *The Parish of St Giles in the Fields*, edited by Gomme and Norman', RIBA *Journal*, XXII, 9 January, p.110
- 'The Architectural Spirit of the Age, text of a paper read before the A.A.', *Builder*, CVIII, 26 February,
- 'The Classical Ideal in Architecture', Text of a paper read before the AA on 22nd February, *Architect and Builders' Journal*, XLI, 3 March, pp.102–3; *Builder*, CVIII, 5 March, pp.215–6
- 'The Architecture of a Railway' (signed AER), *Manchester Guardian*, 6 March
- 'Modernism' (unsigned), *Builder*, CIX, 9 July, pp.23–4
- 'The Watching Loft at St Albans' (AER), *Builder*, CIX, 27 August, p.156
- 'An architect's impressions of Cornwall', *Architects' & Builders Journal*, XLII, 6 October, p.152
- 'Classic Architecture of Russia' Note, *Architects' & Builders Journal*, XLII, 10 November, p.207
- 'Classic Architecture in Russia I', *Architectural Review*, XXXVIII, November, pp.87–99
- 'The Watermen's Hall', *Builder*, CIX, 10 December, p.422
- 'Memorials of War' (AER with RRP – R. Randal Philips); III: 'Napoleonic', *Architectural Review*, XXXVII, pp.62–71; VI: 'Modern British', ibid., pp.96–104; V: 'Modern French', XXXVIII, pp.7–12; VI: 'Modern Italian', ibid., pp.73–8; VII: 'Modern American', ibid., pp.106–13

1916

- 'Classic Architecture in Russia, II, III & IV' (Country Houses), *Architectural Review*, XXXIX, January, pp.19–24; March, pp.50–55; May, pp.95–103
- 'The Development of Cheltenham in the Early 19th Century', *Town Planning Review*, VI, April, pp.227–32
- 'The General Post Office, Dublin', *Architects' & Builders Journal*, XLIII, 10 May, pp.194–5
- 'The Civic Arts Association', *Builder*, CXI, 14 July, p.20
- 'Naval Architecture and Decoration of the past' (AER), *Architectural Review*, XL, July, pp.1–6; August pp.24–9
- 'A Unique Group of Almshouses', *Architect & Builders Journal*, XLIV, 18 October, p.180
- 'Classical Architecture in Trieste', *Architectural Review*, XL, pp.77–80
- 'Old Road Books', *Builder*, CXI, 3 November, p.273
- 'Metal Shop Fronts', *Builder*, CXI, 10 November, p.291
- 'The Arts and Crafts Exhibition', RIBA *Journal*, XXIII, 11 Nov, pp.9–12
- Contribution to debate 'Architecture and Civilisation' at RIBA, RIBA *Journal*, XXIII, 1916, pp.87–9
- 'Here and There' (Ubique), *Architects' & Builders Journal*, XLIV, 22 November, pp.234–5
- 'The County Halls of Chelmsford and Lewes', *Architects' & Builders Journal*, XLIV, 29 November, pp.248–9
- 'The Hampton Court of East London'. Article on Eastbury Manor, *Manchester Guardian*, 14 December
- 'Here and There' (Ubique), *Architect & Builders Journal*, XLIV, 6 December, p.256
- 'The Military Trophy in Architectural Decoration' (AER), *Architectural Review*, XL, December, pp.112–122

1917

- Appreciation of Herbert Batsford (unsigned), *Architects' & Builders Journal*, XLV, 24 January, pp.43–4
- 'A Great Architectural Publisher. Appreciation of Herbert Batsford', *Builder*, CXII, 26 January, p.65
- 'The Small Town House of the Early Regency Period', *Architects' & Builders Journal*, XLV, 31 January, pp.56–8
- 'Small Houses and Cottages at St Albans II', *Architectural Review*, XLII, pp.21–25; 71–80
- 'Education of Architects' [contribution to discussion], *Builder*, CXII, p.147

1918

- 'Reading – a vignette', *Architectural Review*, XLIII, January, pp.2–9
- 'The Architect of Dartmoor' (Daniel Asher Alexander), *Architectural Review*, XLIII, pp.77–80
- 'An impression of Southampton with notes on the church of All Saints', *The Architect*, C, 13 September, pp.141–2
- Designer of Ionic Capital by Professor Cockerell (AER), RIBA *Journal*, XXV, October, p.229
- Review of Guy Lowell's *Villages and Farms of Italy*, RIBA *Journal*, XXV, October, pp.198–203

1919

- 'The Architecture of Southampton', *Architetural Review*, XLV, February, pp.29–37
- Aims and Ambitions; introductory editorial, *Architects' Journal*, XLIX, 5 March, pp.130–1
- 'Architectural Causerie' (AERO), *Architects' Journal*, XLIX, 5 March, p.132
- 'William Paine, Architect and Carpenter', *Architects' Journal*, XLIX, 5 March, pp.134–6
- 'Architectural Causerie' (AERO), *Architects' Journal*, XLIX, 12 March, p.148
- 'Architectural Causerie' (AERO), *Architects' Journal*, XLIX, 19 March, p.166
- 'Bouchet's compositions' (unsigned), *Architects' Journal*, XLIX, 19 March, pp.171–2
- 'Architectural Causerie' (US architecture) (AERO), *Architects' Journal*, XLIX, 26 March, p.182
- 'The Reform of Architectural Education' (editorial, AER), *Architect's Journal*, XLIX, 2 April, pp.197–8
- 'Architectural Causerie' (AERO), *Architects' Journal*, XLIX, 2 April, p.200
- 'Architectural Causerie' (AERO), *Architects' Journal*, XLIX, 9 April, p.216
- 'Architectural Causerie' (AERO), *Architects' Journal*, XLIX, 16 April, p.234
- 'Architectural Causerie' (Fireplaces) (AERO), *Architects' Journal*, XLIX, 23 April, p.254
- 'Architectural Causerie' (AERO), *Architects' Journal*, XLIX, 30 April, p.270
- 'Street Decorations for Peace', *Architects' Journal*, XLIX, 7 May, p.287–8
- 'A Minor town Development Scheme of the Regency', *Architects' Journal*, XLIX, 7 May, p.294

- 'Architectural Causerie' (AERO), *Architects' Journal*, XLIX, 14 May, p.311
- 'Architectural Causerie' (AERO), *Architects' Journal*, XLIX, 21 May, p.335
- Review of *Woodwork in Principle and Practice* by A. Romney Green (AER), *Architectural Review*, XLV, June, pp.131–2
- 'Architectural Causerie' (AERO), *Architects' Journal*, XLIX, 4 June, pp.397–8
- 'Architectural Causerie' (AERO), *Architects' Journal*, XLIX, 11 June, p.433
- 'A Neglected Aspect of the Housing Problem' (AER), *Architects' Journal*, XLIX, 11 June, p.433
- 'Typical Country Towns I., Bourne', *Architects' Journal*, XLIX, 18 June, pp.449–50
- 'Architectural Causerie' (AERO), *Architects' Journal*, XLIX, 18 June, p.451
- 'A Threat to London Bridge', *Architects' Journal*, XLIX, 25 June, p.469
- 'The London and Birmingham Railway' (unsigned), *Architects' Journal*, L, 9 July, pp.41–42
- 'Architectural Causerie' (AERO), *Architects' Journal*, L, 9 July, p.51
- 'Architectural Causerie' (Montagu Town and Buckler's Hard) (AERO), *Architects' Journal*, L, 16 July, pp.81–82
- 'Architectural Causerie' (Isle of Wight) (AERO), *Architects' Journal*, L, 23 July, pp.117–18
- 'Architectural Causerie' (Door Knockers) (AERO), *Architects' Journal*, L, 30 July, pp.141–2
- 'Architectural Causerie' (American Small Houses) (AERO), *Architects' Journal*, L, 6 August, pp.168–70
- 'Architectural Causerie' (Architectural Union Society) (AERO), *Architects' Journal*, L, 13 August, p.202
- 'Architectural Causerie' (AERO), *Architects' Journal*, L, 20 August, p.228
- 'Architectural Causerie' (Wallpaper) (AERO), *Architects' Journal*, L, 27 August, p.258
- 'Architectural Causerie' (Houghton Conquest) (AERO), *Architects' Journal*, L, 3 September, p.288
- 'Architectural Causerie' (Furnishings) (AERO), *Architects' Journal*, L, 10 September, p.318
- 'Architectural Causerie' (London overspill) (AERO), *Architects' Journal*, L, 17 September, p.348
- 'The Rise of Neo-Classic' (editorial, signed AER), *Architects' Journal*, L, 24 September, pp.375–6
- 'Architectural Causerie' (Errors of Taste) (AERO), *Architects' Journal*, L, 24 September, p.378
- 'Architectural Causerie' (Old Shop Fronts, Woburn) (AERO), *Architects' Journal*, L, 1 October, p.408
- 'Architectural Causerie' (New timber-framed housing) (AERO), *Architects' Journal*, L, 8 October, p.438
- 'Architectural Causerie' (Architectural Schools et al.) (AERO), *Architects' Journal*, L, 15 October, p.468
- 'Architectural Causerie' (South Essex) (AERO), *Architects' Journal*, L, 22 October, p.498
- 'Architectural Causerie' (Locks) (AERO), *Architects' Journal*, L, 29 October, p.528
- 'Architectural Causerie' (AERO), *Architects' Journal*, L, 5 November, pp.558–61
- 'Architectural Causerie' (London place names) (AERO), *Architects' Journal*, L, 12 November, p.588
- 'Architectural Causerie' (A New Style) (AERO), *Architects' Journal*, L, 19 November, p.618–20
- 'Architectural Causerie' (London place names) (AERO), *Architects' Journal*, L, 26 November, p.648–51
- 'A Visit to a Country Villa Eighty Years Ago', *Architects' Journal*, L, 3 December, pp.678–82
- 'Architectural Causerie' (Shadow in architectural drawing) (AERO), *Architects' Journal*, L, 3 December, p.687–8
- 'Architectural Causerie' (AERO), *Architects' Journal*, L, 10 December, p.708–11
- 'The Ball Room, Theatre Royal, Plymouth', *Architects' Journal*, L, 10 December, p.717
- Letter signed 'Theophilus Julian', *Architects' Journal*, L, 10 December, p.723
- 'Architectural Causerie' (London Place Names) (AERO), *Architects' Journal*, L, 17 December, p.738–42
- 'Architectural Causerie' (AERO), *Architects' Journal*, L, 24 December, p.768
- 'Architectural Causerie' (London signs) (AERO), *Architects' Journal*, L, 31 December, p.797–8

1920

- 'The charm of the country town: Spalding, Lincolnshire', *Architectural Review*, XLVII, January, pp.1–6
- 'Architectural Causerie' (AERO), *Architects' Journal*, LI, 7 January, p.6
- 'Architectural Causerie' (AERO), *Architects' Journal*, LI, 14 January, p.40
- 'Architectural Causerie' (AERO), *Architects' Journal*, LI, 28 January, p.74
- 'Architectural Causerie: On Cornices' (AERO), *Architects' Journal*, LI, 4 February, p.108
- 'The Architecture of St Neot's', *Architects' Journal*, LI, 4 February, pp.145–6
- 'Architectural Causerie: On Bollards' (AERO), *Architects' Journal*, LI, 11 February, p.176
- 'Classic Architecture in the West of England' *Architects' Journal*, LI, 11 February, p.179
- 'Architectural Causerie: On Lighthouses' (AERO), *Architects' Journal*, LI, 18 February
- 'Architectural Causerie: On roads' (AERO), *Architects' Journal*, LI, 25 February, p.244
- 'Architectural Causerie: Garden Ornaments' (AERO), *Architects' Journal*, LI, 3 March, p.276
- 'Some interesting Southampton buildings', *Architects' Journal*, LI, 3 March, p.279
- 'The Charm of the Country Town – The City of Exeter I', *Architectural Review*, XLVII, March, pp.63–8; April, pp.89–94
- 'Architectural Causerie: Architectural Models' (AERO), *Architects' Journal*, LI, 10 March, p.310
- 'Architectural Causerie: Cornices' (AERO), *Architects' Journal*, LI, 17 March, p.340
- 'Architectural Causerie: Back to Simplicity' (AERO), *Architects' Journal*, LI, 24 March, p.379
- 'Architectural Causerie: Working Methods' (AERO), *Architects' Journal*, LI, 31 March, p.409
- 'Architectural Causerie: The First R.A. Professor of Architecture' (AERO), *Architects' Journal*, LI, 7 April, p.435
- 'Architectural Causerie: Thames Bridges and Embankment' (AERO), *Architects' Journal*, LI, 14 April, p.470

- 'Architectural Causerie: Clocks and Cases' (AERO), *Architects' Journal*, LI, 21 April, p.516
- 'The Future of Architecture (extracts from a paper read before the Architectural Association of Ireland)', *'Architects' Journal*, LI, 21 April, p.523, 28 April, p.562
- 'Architectural Causerie: Dublin Revisited' (AERO), *Architects' Journal*, LI, 28 April, p.561
- 'Architectural Causerie: Architectural Models' (AERO), *Architects' Journal*, LI, 5 May, p.582
- 'Architectural Causerie: On Transport' (AERO), *Architects' Journal*, LI, 12 May, p.616
- 'Architectural Causerie: City Churches' (AERO), *Architects' Journal*, LI, 19 May, p.646
- 'Architectural Causerie: On Housing' (AERO), *Architects' Journal*, LI, 26 May, p.669–70
- 'Architectural Causerie: On Criticism' (AERO), *Architects' Journal*, LI, 2 June, p.704
- 'Architectural Causerie: On Thatching' (AERO), *Architects' Journal*, LI, 9 June, p.726
- 'Architectural Causerie: The English Hostelry' (AERO), *Architects' Journal*, LI, 16 June, p.753
- 'Architectural Causerie: On Windmills' (AERO), *Architects' Journal*, LI, 23 June, p.781–2
- 'Architectural Causerie: On Colour' (AERO), *Architects' Journal*, LI, 30 June, p.809
- 'Daniel Asher Alexander', *Architects' Journal*, LI, 30 June, p.810
- 'Architectural Causerie' (Signing Buildings) (AERO), *Architects' Journal*, LII, 7 July
- 'Daniel Asher Alexander', *Architects' Journal*, LII, 7 July, pp.11–12
- 'Architectural Causerie: The King's Highway' (AERO), *Architects' Journal*, LII, 14 July, p.33
- 'Architectural Causerie: The King's Highway' (AERO), *Architects' Journal*, LII, 21 July, p.61
- 'Architectural Causerie: Thomas Bewick' (AERO), *Architects' Journal*, LII, 28 July,
- 'Architectural Causerie: Thomas Bewick'(AERO), *Architects' Journal*, LII, 4 August, p.124
- 'Architectural Causerie: On Shingles' (AERO), *Architects' Journal*, LII, 11 August, p.145
- 'Architectural Causerie: A Forgotten Architect' (AERO), *Architects' Journal*, LII, 18 August, pp.175–6
- 'Architectural Causerie: East of the Tower' (AERO), *Architects' Journal*, LII, 25 August, p.201
- 'Architectural Causerie: East of the Tower' (AERO), *Architects' Journal*, LII, 1 September, p.229
- 'Architectural Causerie: Notable Lighthouses' (AERO), *Architects' Journal*, LII, 8 September, p.255
- 'The Charm of the Country Town – Monumental Architecture at Plymouth', *Architectural Review*, XLVIII, September, pp.55–9
- 'Architectural Causerie: E.A. Rickards' (AERO), *Architects' Journal*, LII, 15 September, p.283
- 'Architectural Causerie: Notable Lighthouses' (AERO), *Architects' Journal*, LII, 22 September, p.311
- 'Architectural Causerie: Anecdotes' (AERO), *Architects' Journal*, LII, 29 September, pp.340–1
- 'Architectural Causerie: Scottish Impressions' (AERO), *Architects' Journal*, LII, 6 October, p.367
- 'Architectural Causerie: Irish Impressions' (AERO), *Architects' Journal*, LII, 13 October, pp.395–6
- 'Architectural Causerie: Italian Villas' (AERO), *Architects' Journal*, LII, 20 October, p.423
- 'Architectural Causerie: Buontalenti's Villas' (AERO), *Architects' Journal*, LII, 27 October, pp.454–5
- 'Architectural Causerie: More Italian Villas' (AERO), *Architects' Journal*, LII, 3 November, p.481
- 'Architectural Causerie: Smeaton and James' (AERO), *Architects' Journal*, LII, 10 November, p.508
- 'Architectural Causerie: Soane and the Bank' (AERO), *Architects' Journal*, LII, 17 November, p.537
- 'Architectural Causerie: About the Albert Hall' (AERO), *Architects' Journal*, LII, 24 November, p.565
- 'Architectural Causerie: About the Albert Hall' (AERO), *Architects' Journal*, LII, 1 December, p.593
- 'Architectural Causerie: Modern Opinion' (AERO), *Architects' Journal*, LII, 8 December, p.621
- 'Architectural Causerie: About the Scillies I' (AERO), *Architects' Journal*, LII, 15 December, p.649
- 'Library Architecture' (extracts from a lecture delivered at University College), *Architects' Journal*, LII, 15 December, p.663
- 'Architectural Causerie: About the Scillies' (AERO), *Architects' Journal*, LII, 22 December, p.676
- 'Architectural Causerie: The Eighteenth century in London' (AERO), *Architects' Journal*, LII, 29 December, p.707
- 'Southampton', *Town Planning Review*, VIII, pp.69–78

1921

- 'Architectural Causerie: Railway Practice' (AERO), *Architects' Journal*, LIII, 5 January, p.6
- 'Architectural Causerie: Concerning Libraries' (AERO), *Architects' Journal*, LIII, 12 January, p.34
- 'Architectural Causerie: English Libraries' (AERO), *Architects' Journal*, LIII, 19 January, p.63
- 'Architectural Causerie: Untidiness' (AERO), *Architects' Journal*, LIII, 26 January, p.91
- 'The Charm of the Country Town – Boston, Lincolnshire', *Architectural Review*, XLIX, February, pp.35–42
- 'Architectural Causerie: An American Critic' (AERO), *Architects' Journal*, LIII, 2 February, pp.117–8
- 'Architectural Causerie: Eighteenth century fireplaces' (AERO), *Architects' Journal*, LIII, 9 February, p.151
- 'Architectural Causerie: Eighteenth century fireplaces' (AERO), *Architects' Journal*, LIII, 16 February, p.182
- 'Architectural Causerie: George Papworth' (AERO), *Architects' Journal*, LIII, 23 February, p.212
- 'The Design of Banking Premises' (AERO), *Architects' Journal*, LIII, 2 March, pp.233–9
- 'Architectural Causerie: The Chippendales' (AERO), *Architects' Journal*, LIII, 9 March, p.288
- 'Architectural Causerie: The Chippendales' (AERO), *Architects' Journal*, LIII, 16 March
- 'Architectural Causerie: The Chippendales' (AERO), *Architects' Journal*, LIII, 23 March, p.343

- 'The Building Trades Exhibition: A Plea for Improved Planning', *Architects' Journal*, LIII, 13 April, p.462
- 'Architectural Causerie', *Architects' Journal*, LIII, 27 April, p.523
- 'Architectural Causerie: The Sordid Side' (AERO), *Architects' Journal*, LIII, 11 May, p.580
- 'Architectural Causerie', *Architects' Journal*, LIII, 18 May, p.609
- 'Architectural Causerie: Where tradition lingers' (AERO), *Architects' Journal*, LIII, 1 June, p.669
- 'The Charm of the Country Town VI – Ampthill, Bedfordshire', *Architectural Review*, L, July, pp.5–9; August, pp.44–46, October, pp.92–6
- 'Architectural Causerie – Northampton: An impression' (AERO), *Architects' Journal*, LIV, 24 August, pp.217–8
- 'The Architecture of Newport Pagnell' (AERO), *Architects' Journal*, LIV, 7 September, pp.275–6
- 'The Charm of the Country Town. King's Lynn, Norfolk', *Architectural Review*, LII, July, pp.5–11

1923

- Book review of *The Furniture of Duncan Fyfe* by Charles Cornelius Over, February
- 'Library Architecture', *Library Association Record*, June
- 'The Renewal of Vitality in Building' (paper given before the Architectural Association), *Architects' Journal*, LV, 23 January, pp.192–3, *Builder*, CXXIV, 18 January, pp.104–5
- 'As Others See Us', *Builder*, CXXIV, 9 February, p.231
- 'London Brickwork', *Builder*, CXXV, 14 September, pp.409–10
- 'Late Georgian: Its values and Limitations', *Architecture* (Journal of the Society of Architects), pp.545–7
- 'Parish Church, Harlington, *Builder*, CXXV, 30 November
- 'Sir Christopher Wren's Public Buildings' in *Sir Christopher Wren, Bi-centenary memorial volume*, general editor, Rudolf Dircks, 1924
- *Regional Architecture of the West of England* (with C. Lovett Gill), Ernest Benn Ltd.
- 'Liverpool Cathedral', *Evening Sun* (Baltimore, USA)
- Review of Survey of London, St Leonard's, Shoreditch, RIBA *Journal*, XXX, p.497

1924

- 'The First Principles of Building', *Architecture*, II, 1923–4, pp.604–9
- 'The Modern Movement in Architecture, RIBA *Journal*, Series 3, XXXI, pp.267–74; *Builder*, CXXVI, 29 February, pp.342–3
- Review of *Domestic Architecture in the American Colonies of the Early Republic*, RIBA *Journal*, XXXI, p.461
- Review of Survey of London, Vol.IX, RIBA *Journal*, XXXI, p.669
- 'A Discussion of Principles for Future Building' (paper before Pembroke College, Cambridge), *Builder*, CXXVI, 7 March, pp.384–5
- 'Present-Day Architecture' (paper before the Architecture Club), *Builder*, CXXVI, 7 March, p.681
- The London University School of Architecture, *Architects Journal*, LX, 30 July, p.161
- 'Waterloo Bridge. Some notes on John Rennie's masterpiece' *Architects' Journal*, LIX, 2 April, pp.553–8

1925

- *The English Inn Past and Present. A Review of its History and Social Life.* (with H. Donaldson Eberlin), London, B.T. Batsford Ltd.
- *The Smaller English House of the Later Renaissance 1660–1830, An account of its design plan and details*, London, B.T. Batsford Ltd.
- Introduction to *Changing London* (second series) by Hanslip Fletcher, London, Cassell & Co.
- 'London Past and Present', *Builder*, CXXVIII, 6 March, p.384
- 'At the Royal Academy', *Architectural Review*, LVII, June, pp.256–7
- Letter to the Editor 'The Eighth Lamp' by 'E. Massingham Warboys' (pseud. AER), *Architecture*, IV, pp.95–6
- 'English Towns I: Lymington, Hampshire', *Architecture*, IV, pp.79–80
- 'English Towns II: Brighton', *Architecture*, IV, pp.144–6
- 'English Towns III: Bury St Edmunds', *Architecture*, IV, pp.204–6
- 'English Towns IV: Alnwick', *Architecture*, IV, p.232
- 'The Relationship between construction and design in Architecture', *Builder*, CXXIX, 23 October, p.599

1926

- 'New Work by Sir Edwin Lutyens', *Architects' Journal*, LXIII, 6 January, pp.15–27
- 'Bourne's Drawings', *Architecture*, IV, pp.294–6
- 'Highgate', *Architecture*, IV, p.318
- 'The Training of an Architect and National Architecture', *Irish Builder and Engineer*, 20 March, pp.205–10
- 'Architecture fom the Structural Point of View' (paper before Institute of Technology, Manchester), RIBA *Journal*, 20 March, pp.159–65; *Builder*, CXXX, 19 February, p.320; *Structural Engineer*, May, pp.159–65
- 'The Training of an Architect and National Architecture', *Builder*, CXXX, 12 March, p.426
- 'An Unknown Wren Church in Buckinghamshire', *English Life*, June, pp.6–10
- 'The New University', *New Troy*, 17 June, pp.109–110
- 'The Royal Pavilion at Weedon – an echo of 1803', *English Life*, pp.13–15
- 'The Cathedral of St. Sophia, Bayswater, *Architecture*, IV, pp.236–9

1927

- 'Correspondence' (St George's Hall and the Proposed Cenotaph), *Builder*, CXXXII, 8 April, p.556
- 'Modern Street Architecture' (paper before the London Society), *Builder*, CXXXII, 6 May, p.739
- 'Houghton House, Ampthill, Bedfordshire', *Builder*, CXXXII, 24 June
- 'Snowshill Manor', *Country Life*, LXII, 1 October, pp.470–77

1928

- 'The Way We Are Going', *Building*, July, p.300
- *Changing London* (third series), A Book of Sketches by Hanslip Fletcher with an introduction and notes by Professor A.E. Richardson, London, Methuen & Co.
- 'Modernism in Architecture', RIBA *Journal*, XXXV, June, (AER's contribution to debate, pp.518–9
- *Georgian England, A Survey of Social Life, Trades, Industries and Art from 1700 to 1820*, London, B.T. Batsford Ltd.

1929

- 'Modern English Architecture', *Journal of the Royal Society of Arts*, 24 May, pp.696–707; *Builder*, CXXXVI, pp.603–4
- Introduction to *Changing London* (Third Series) by Hanslip Fletcher, London Methuen & Co.
- Introduction to *Plates of Building Construction* by Walter Robert Jaggard, London, Architectural Press
- 'English Architecture', *Builder*, CXXXVI, pp.503; 648
- 'The English Road', *Builder*, CXXXVI, p.734
- 'Buildings of the Later Renaissance in France', *Builder*, CXXXVI, p.1171

1930

- 'Architects' Drawings 1800–1851 (paper before the RIBA), *Builder*, CXXXVIII, 2 May, pp.846–7
- 'Aims and Ambitions' (paper before the Royal Society of Arts), *Builder*, CXXXIX, 21 November, p.869
- 'Making a Nation of Neighbours', *Daily Herald*, 4 April

1931

- 'The Collector 9: Farmhouse Bygones', *Countryman*, V, April, p.113
- 'The Snobbery of Being Different', *Master Builder*, CXLI, June, p.17
- 'The Collector 10: Bottles & Scales', *Countryman*, V, July, p.351
- 'The Collector 11: Models of Country Houses and Carriages, *Countryman*, V, October, pp.571–3
- 'Art of Today', *Builder*, CXLI, 6 November, p.754
- 'Modern Decoration', *Builder*, CXLI, 4 December, p.924

1932

- 'Country Buildings', *Builder*, CXLII, 5 February, p.274
- 'The Collector 12: Warming Pans', *Countryman*, V, January, p.772
- 'The Collector 13: Coaching Prints', *Countryman*, VI, April, p.133
- 'The Collector: Pictures of Old and New', *Countryman*, VI, July, p.415
- 'The Collector: Tea-katis & Tea-poys', *Countryman*, VI, October, p.717

1933

- 'A Licensed Life for Buildings' (letter), *Architect & Building News*, CXXIII, p.154
- 'A Visit to Sweden', *Builder*, CXLIV, 13 January, pp.52–4
- The Collector 15: Domestic Silver', *Countryman*, VI, January, pp.907–11
- 'Must the Adelphi go?', *Architectural Review*, LXXIII, March, pp.99–100
- 'The Collector 16: Looking Glasses and Mirrors', *Countryman*, VI, April, p.105
- 'A trip to Cambridge', *Builder*, CXLIV, pp.994–5
- 'The Collector 17: Illustrations of Country Life', *Countryman*, July, p.449
- 'Is Modern Architecture on the Right Track?', *Listener*, 25 July, p.126
- 'Knotting Church', *Bedfordshire Times*
- 'The Collector 18: Garrard – Animal Sculptor', *Countryman*, VII, October, p.79

1934

- *The Old Inns of England* (with a foreword by Sir Edwin Lutyens, RA, illustrated with drawings by Brian Cook and from photographs). London, B.T. Batsford Ltd.
- 'Architecture' in *Early Victorian England*, ed. G.M. Young, Vol.II, pp.179–247, Oxford University Press
- 'The Collector 19: Old Games', *Countryman*, VIII, January, pp.443–5
- 'The Collector 20: Ornamental and Useful', *Countryman*, IX, April, p.155–7
- 'The Collector 22: Decorative Needlework', *Countryman*, X, October, p.233–7
- 'Centenary Reminiscences 1834–1934', *Builder*, CXLVI, pp.747–50

1935

- 'The Collector 23: Boxes, Odd and Curious', *Countryman*, X, January, p.563
- 'The Collector 24: Miniatures', *Countryman*, XI, April, p.229
- 'The Collector 25: Old Knives and Forks', *Countryman*, XI, July, p.585
- 'The Collector 26: Eastern Rugs', *Countryman*, XII, October, p.179

1936

- 'Erewhon come True', pp.111–49, in *The Seven Pillars of Fire, A Symposium* [on the state of the contemporary world by Dr. Maude Royden, Dr. L.P. Jacks, Prof. A.E. Richardson, the Marquis of Tavistock, C.W.R. Nevinson, Capt. Bernard Acworth and Sir E. Dennison Ross, London, Herbert Jenkins]
- 'The Collector 27: Old Glass', *Countryman*, XII, January, p.524
- 'The Collector 28: Cupboards and Shelves', *Countryman*, April, p.229
- 'The Collector 29: Figurants', *Countryman*, XIII, July, p.659
- 'The Collector 30: Screens, 1700–1850', *Countryman*, XIV, October, pp.231–3

1937

- 'Correspondence' ('Reigns and Styles'), *Builder*, CLII, 8 January, p.64
- 'The Collector 31: The Fireside', *Countryman*, XIV, January, p.653
- 'The Art of Architecture' (lecture before Manchester University), *Builder*, CLII, 30 April, p.938
- 'The Collector 32: Regency Garnitures', *Countryman*, XV, April, p.247
- 'The Collector 33: Settees and Sofas', *Countryman*, XV, July, p.647
- 'The Collector 34: Odds and Ends', *Countryman*, XVI, October, p.217
- 'The Gothic Revival of the Early 19th Century', RIBA *Journal*, XLV, 6 December, pp.140–1

1938

- *The Art of Architecture* (with Hector Corfiato), Foreword by Profesor W.G. Constable. London, The English University Presses Ltd. (reprinted 1946 and 1952)
- 'The Collector 35: More Oddments', *Countryman*, XVI, January, p.608
- 'The Collector 36: Locks and Keys', *Countryman*, XVII, April, pp.199–200
- 'The Collector 37: Famous Victorians', *Countryman*, XVII, July, p.607
- 'The Collector 38: Salt Glaze Ware', *Countryman*, XVIII, October, p.221–2
- 'The Charm of Old London', *Listener*, 23 February, pp.405–7

1939

- 'The Collector 39: Old French Prints', *Countryman*, XVIII, January, p.225
- 'Recent Achievements in European Architecture' (paper to Architectural Association), *Architectural Association Journal*, LIV, April, pp.231–43, letter from Gerhard Kallmann, student, p.274
- 'Railway Stations' (paper before RIBA), RIBA *Journal*, XLVI, 8 May, pp.645–60; *Builder*, CLVI, 31 October, pp.790–2

1940

- Foreword to *Purbeck Shop* by Eric Benfield, Oxford University Press
- Illustrations to article, 'The Age-Old Battlefield' by W.E. Barber, *Country Life*, CLXXXVII, 1 June, pp.544–5
- 'A Disquisition on Perambulators', *Country Life*, 9 November, pp.408–9

1941

- 'The Philosophy of Building Repair' (lecture at New College, Oxford), *Builder*, CXL, 14 March, pp.266–7
- Correspondence 'Strange Proposals', *Builder*, CLXI, 12 December, p.526

1942

- Obituary for Sir Edwin Cooper, RA (Richardson also contributed the entry on Cooper to the DNB)
- 'Old Towns Re-visited – III: Berwick-on-Tweed', *Country Life*, XCI, 10 April, pp.704–6
- 'Architecture, Craftsmanship and the Public', *Art & Reason*, May 1942, pp.1–3

1943

- 'The English Town' (lecture to the Georgian Group), *Builder*, CLXV, 21 May, p.458
- 'The Rural Housing Problem', *Country Life*, XCIV, pp.898–900
- 'Raising the Standard of Public Taste', *Art & Industry*, December, pp.162–8

1944

- 'London Rebuilt', *Cambridge Review*, 22 January, pp.152–4
- 'Our Heritage in the City Churches', *Friends of the City Churches*, Occasional Paper, No.1, 1944, pp.5–16
- Review of *Greek and Roman Architecture*, *Classical Review*, LVIII, No.2, December

1945

- 'The Heritage of the Copy-Book', *Art & Reason*, pp.1–3
- 'Architects' Copy Books', *Country Life*, XCVIII, 26 October, pp.732–3

1946

- 'Character in Architecture', *Art & Reason*, August, pp.3–5
- Preface to *Decorative Details of the Eighteenth Century by William and James Pain*, London, A. Tiranti

1947

- 'The Visual Arts', in *The Character of England*, edited by Sir Ernest Barker, Oxford University Press, Chapter XVII, pp.367–388
- Introduction to *Bombed London* by Hanslip Fletcher, London, Cassell & Co.
- 'Convention and Convenience', *Builder*, CLXXII, p.505
- 'Tradition', *Art & Reason*, February, pp.7–9
- 'The Architecture of London', *Art & Reason*, May 1947, pp.2–4
- 'The Character of London's Architecture' *Royal Institution of Great Britain Journal*, March
- 'The Architecture of London', *Art & Reason*, July, pp.7–10
- Georgian Ampthill, *Bedfordshire Magazine*, Vol.1, pp.3–7
- 'Architecture and the Crafts', *Art & Reason*, December, pp.1–5
- Speech on receiving RIBA Royal Gold Medal, RIBA *Journal*, May, p.357
- 'Convention and Convenience' (Bossom Gift lecture of the Chadwick Trust at University College), *Builder*, CLXXII, 1947, 23 May, pp.505–7

1948

- *Design in Civil Architecture, Volume 1: Elevational Treatments* (with Hector Corfiato), London, The English Universities Press Ltd.
- Introduction to *The Student's Letrarouilly*, London, Alec Tiranti Ltd.
- 'Architecture and the Crafts', *Art & Reason*, January, pp.1–5
- 'Architecture and the Crafts', *Art & Reason*, February, pp.1–3
- 'The Renaissance in England', *Norwich Arts Federation Bulletin*, No.3
- 'Architecture and the Crafts', *Quarterly of the Royal Incorporation of Architects in Scotland*, February, pp.6–14
- 'Highgate', an address given at Cromwell House, 17 July, *Mothercraft Training Society*
- Ampthill Park, *Bedfordshire Magazine*, Vol.1, pp.234–5
- 'Riverside Gleanings', *Builder*, CLXXIV, 9 January, pp.38–41
- 'The Spirit of British Craftsmanship' (Peter Le Neve Foster Lecture to the Royal Society of Arts), *Architects' Journal*, 1 July; *Builder*, CLXXIV, p.738
- 'Georgian Art and Architecture' (address to the Council for Visual Education), *Builder*, CLXXIV, 1948, pp.108–9

1949

- *An Introduction to Georgian Architecture*, London, Art & Technics.
- 'Homage to the carriers', *Bedfordshire Magazine*, Vol.1, pp.294–6
- 'An early school of needlework at Ampthill', *Bedfordshire Magazine*, Vol.2, pp.11–13
- 'LCC Housing, First Opinions', *Architects' Journal*, 19 May, p.451
- 'Architectural Education: 'Something is rotten in the state of Denmark', *Builder*, CLXXVII, 15 July, pp.68–9
- 'World Portents', *Builder*, CLXXVII, 19 August, p.223
- 'Plymouth: Some Thoughts on its Future', *Builder*, CLXXVII, 23 September, pp.380–1

1950

- 'The Majesty of London' (address to the London and district Branch of Incorporated Accountants), *Builder*, CLXXVIII, pp.108–9
- 'Festival of Britain Competition Designs', *Building*, XXV, February, pp.44–9
- 'The Future of Bristol' (address to the Bristol and Somerset Society), *Builder*, CLXXVIII, 3 March, pp.299–300
- 'Time, Gentlemen, Time', *Building*, XXV, May, p.167
- 'Social Culture and the Arts of Decoration', *The Record Journal of the Incorporated Institute of British Decorators*, September, pp.37–45
- 'Organisation of Architects' Offices 10: The Office of A.E. Richardson, RA, FRIBA', *Builder*, CLXXVIII, 23 June, p.835

1951

- 'The House' in *Southill, A Regency House*, Faber & Faber Ltd., London, pp.1–17
- Review of *Henry Holland, 1745–1806*, by Dorothy Stroud, RIBA *Journal*, January, p.115
- 'English Art and Architecture: 1751–90' (lecture to the Royal Society), *Builder*, CLXXX, 16 March, p.391
- 'The Arts in 1951', *Building*, XXV, July, pp.272–3
- 'The Gentle Art of Making Enemies', *Building*, XXV, August, pp.304–5
- 'The Difficult Art of Making Friends', *Building*, XXV, September, p.347
- 'Novelty', *Building*, XXV, October, p.385
- 'The Eighth Lamp', *Building*, XXV, November, p.427
- 'London Skyscrapers', *Building*, XXV, December, p.469

1952

- 'Vitruvius Redivivus', *Building*, XXVI, January, p.15
- 'On Making Things Look Modern', XXVI, *Building*, March, p.93
- 'Comparisons', *Building*, XXVI, April, p.133
- 'Art Exhibitions', *Building*, XXVI, May, p.209
- 'Manners in Creative Art', *Building*, XXVI, July, p.256
- 'For Reviving the Arts', *Building*, XXVI, August, pp.189–191
- 'Cause and Effect', *Building*, XXVI, September, p.326
- 'The Boomerang', *Building*, XXVI, October, p.368
- 'Rebuilding London', *Building*, XXVI, November, p.410
- 'A Misconception of Luxury', *Building*, XXVI, December, p.448

1953

- 'Everybody's Measuring Scale', *Building*, XXVII, January, p.14
- 'The Contemporary Manner', *Building*, XXVII, February, p.50
- 'The Period of Transition', *Building*, XXVII, March, pp.89–90
- 'Decoration and Colour', *Building*, XXVII, April, p.128–9
- 'Architecture and Needlework', *Building*, XXVII, May, pp.175–6
- 'Coronation Decoration', *Building*, XXVII, June, pp.204–5
- 'The Age of Steam', *Building*, XXVII, July, p.246
- 'National Parks and Landscape Preservation', *Building*, XXVII, August, p.290
- 'The Status of the Architect', *Building*, XXVII, September, p.328
- 'Smog', *Building*, XXVII, October, p.411
- 'Exhibitionism', *Building*, XXVII, November, p.453

1954

- The Oliver Sheldon Memorial Lecture – A Centre of Architecture in York, York, 17 March (pamphlet)
- 'Shops and Shopkeeping Through the Ages', *Journal of the Royal Society of Arts*, 25 June, pp.610–27
- San Pedro de Roma Por Letrarouilly, Prologo por el Professor A.E. Richardson, *Arquitectura*, La Habana, February, pp.48–54
- 'Posterity and the Arts', *Architecture & Building*, XXVIII, January, p.12
- 'Rebuilding the City', *Architecture & Building*, XXVIII, February, pp.55–6

1955

- *Robert Mylne, Architect and Engineer 1733 to 1811*, London, B.T. Batsford Ltd.
- 'The Rebuilding of London', *Architect & Building News*, CCVIII, pp.104–7; *Builder*, CLXXXIX, p.187
- 'The Reaction Against Modernism', *Illustrated London News*, 20 August, p.320
- *Scholarship and the Fine Arts*, The Foundation Oration, Birkbeck College, pp.3–13

1956

- 'Why is civic design neglected?' *Journal of the Town Planning Institute*, XLII, March 1956, pp.78–84; *Builder*, CXC, 13 April, p.305

1957

- 'The Visual Arts and Imaginative Literature' Chapter IV (pp.66–84) in The New Cambridge Modern History, Vol.VII, *The Old Regime 1713–63*, Cambridge, at the University Press
- Foreword (pp.ix-x) to *William Richard Lethaby 1857–1931. A volume in honour of the School's first Principal prepared by A.R.N. Roberts at the suggestion of William Johnstone* OBE, London County Council, Central School of Arts and Crafts
- 'Ampthill is the Spirit of Many Englands', *Luton News*, 30 May, 6 June
- Review of *English Country Houses, Mid-Georgian*, by Christopher Hussey, RIBA *Journal*, April, pp.235–6

1958

- 'The Pursuit of Happiness' in *My Philosophy of Life*, A Symposum edited by the Rt. Honourable Lord Inman, PC, JP, FRSH, Odhams Press, Ltd., London, pp.150–74

1962

- 'A Painter's Views on Architecture' (Francis Grant PRA and Burlington House), *Country Life*, CXXXII, 8 July, p.14

1963

- 'A 17th century Admiral's Staircase' (Manor House, N. Walsham, Norfolk), *Country Life*, CXXXIII, 23 May, p.1167
- 'Impressionism – The Root of all Fine Art', *Glasgow Illustrated*, November, pp.46–7

FANTASY DRAWINGS

(published in the *Builder*, 1928–1936)

- Tower of Babble, CXXXIV, 1928, p.63
- Old St Paul's, CXXXVI, 1929, p.79
- York, a microcosm, CXXXVI, 1929, p.1075
- Spanish Fantasy, CXXXVIII, 1930, p.75
- Dance of Life, CXXXVIII, 1930, p.346
- Road to Norwich, CXXXVIII, 1930, p.1176
- 'Progress', a satire, CXL, 1931, p.69
- Festival of St Valentine, CXL, 1931, p.321
- Feast of the Blessed Virgin: A Fantasy (colour plate), CXLII, 1932, p.66
- England in the Nineteenth Century 'Springtime', CXLII, 1932, p.309
- England in the Nineteenth Century 'Summer 1851', CXLII, 1932, p.973
- England in the Nineteenth Century 'Autumn 1885', CXLIII, 1932, p.640
- England in the Nineteenth Century 'Winter 1900', CXLIII, 1932, p.936
- 'Feast of the Guilds' A Fantasy of the 16th century, CXLIV, 1933, p.98
- Fantasy of the Early 16th century, CXLVI, 1934, p.59
- 'Turn of the Tide' A fantasy of the 16th century, CXLVIII, 1935, p.67

- Fleet Street, Ludgate Hill and Old St Paul's, 1664, CXLVIII, 1935, p.214
- Fantasy of the 16th century, CL, 1936, p.69

BROADCASTS

- Third Programme, 25 September 1947: 'The Visual Arts' (discussion of architectural education with Maxwell Fry and Ian McCallum)
- Home Service, 21 March 1948: The Critics: 'The Plan for Westminster'
- Light Programme, 9 December 1954: The Harding Interview (Gilbert Harding)
- Home Service, 11 March 1955: 'At Home and Abroad': London development plans
- Home Service, 27 April 1955: Speech at RA dinner
- 'London Calling Asia', 18 April 1955: 'Personal Call' (interviewed by Stephen Black)
- Home Service, 10 December 1955: 'In Town Tonight' (Re-election as PRA)
- General Overseas Service, 13 March 1956, Report from South East Bedfordshire
- Home Service, 8 April 1956: 'Time Travellers: England in the 18th century'
- Home Service, 31 May 1956: 'Frankly Speaking' (Interviewed by John Betjeman, Margaret Lane and Lionel Hall)
- Home Service, 23 December 1956 'Conversation Piece' (AER and John Betjeman)
- BBC Television, 9 January 1957: 'At Home: Sir Albert Richardson' (commentator Hywel Davies)
- Home Service, 2 April 1963: 'The Masters' Thomas Hardy (repeat of part of Betjeman conversation)

OBITUARIES

- National papers: *The Times*, 4 February 1964; *Daily Telegraph*, 3 February 1964
- Specialised journals: *Architect & Building News*, CCXXV, pp.218, 255–6; *Architects' Journal, Architectural Association Journal*, March 1964 (George Balcombe), *Builder*, CCVI, 7 February 1964, pp.273–4
- Local papers: *Bath & Wilts Evening Chronicle*, 3 and 5 February 1964; *Bedfordshire Times*, 7 February 1964; *Middlesex City Times*, 8 February 1964; *Nottingham Journal*, 4 February 1964

BOOKS AND ARTICLES

- *Sir Albert Richardson, KCVO, PPRA, FRIBA, FSA, Hon MA (Cantab), Hon Litt.D. (Dublin), Hon RWS 1880–1964* Private publication edited by J. Lawson Petingale, MRSL, n.d. *c.*1964, including addresses by Charles Wheeler, D.B. Harris (former Vicar of Holy Cross, Greenford), tributes by John Betjeman, Michael Wharton (Peter Simple), James Wentworth Day, and James Lees-Milne, texts of addresses by Richardson to Ealing Arts Club, and essay 'The Renewal of the Arts Today'. Copy in Bedford Record Office
- Nicholas Taylor, 'A Classic Case of Edwardianism' *Architectural Review*, CLV, 1966 (September), pp.299–205, reprinted in Alastair Service, *Edwardian Architecture and its Origins*, London, Architectural Press, 1975, pp.444–59
- *Compositions in Perspective. Designs by Noted Architects of the Past lent by Mrs Eric Houfe from the Collection of Sir Albert Richardson* (ed. S.R. Houfe), Cecil Higgins Gallery, Bedford, 1967
- *Architectural Drawings from the Collection of Sir Albert Richardson*, Department of Fine Art, University of Nottingham, 1968 (Foreword by Alastair Smart, Introduction by John Wilton-Ely)
- Simon Houfe, 'The Architectural Work of Sir Albert Richardson in Bedfordshire, 1919–64', *Bedfordshire Magazine*, XIII, 1972, pp.176–83
- Simon Houfe, *Sir Albert Richardson. The Professor*, Luton, White Crescent Press Ltd., 1980
- Kathleen Byers Richardson, *Moving In*, Bedford, 1985
- Dr Ian Toplis, 'Sir Albert Richardson in Wendover: A Microcosm of an Architectural Career', *Records of Buckinghamshire*, XXII, 1990, pp.137–46
- Carolyn Pope, *Sir Albert Richardson, KCVO, PPRA, His Sources of inspiration, principles and architecture.* Thesis submitted for Diploma in Architecture, Thames Polytechnic, Dartford, 1987
- Simon Houfe, 'Putting the Clock Back at Christmas: Recollections of Ampthill', *Country Life*, 1 December, 1988, pp.194–9

AVENUE HOUSE, AMPTHILL

- *Country Life*, 2 December, 1922, pp.744–7; 8 December, 1934, pp.614–9; *House & Garden*, XIII, 1958, pp.76–81

REFERENCE BOOK ENTRIES

- *Dictionary of National Biography, 1961–70*, Oxford University Press, 1981, pp.878–80 (Sir John Summerson)
- *Macmillan Encyclopedia of Architects*, 1982, Vol.III, pp.556–7 (Gavin Stamp)
- *Dictionary of Art*, London, Macmillan, 1996, Vol.XXVI, pp.336–7 (Alan Powers)

Notes and References

'A VINDICATION OF CLASSICAL PRINCIPLES': ALBERT RICHARDSON AND HIS HISTORICAL SOURCES PAGES 9–21

In addition to the benefit of several years of conversations with Sir Albert Richardson himself, the author is also greatly indebted, in the preparation of this text, to Sir Albert's daughter, the late Mrs Kathleen Houfe, his son-in-law and partner, the late Mr Eric Houfe, and, more recently and even more extensively, to his grandson, Mr Simon Houfe.

1. D. Watkin, *The Rise of Architectural History*, London, Architectural Press, 1980, p.120.
2. In Richardson's annotated copy of Reynolds's *Discourses on Art*, bracketing and heavy underlining are given to all the passages expressing this fundamental belief. A characteristic passage is: 'we must have recourse to the Ancients as instructors. It is from a careful study of their works that you will be enabled to attain to the real simplicity of nature; they will suggest many observations that would probably escape you, if your study were confined to nature alone. And, indeed, I cannot help suspecting that, in this instance, the ancients had an easier task than the Moderns. They had, probably, little or nothing to unlearn, as their manners were nearly approaching to this desirable simplicity [AER's underlining]; while the modern artist, before he can see the truth of things, is obliged to remove a veil, with which the fashion of the times has thought proper to cover her.' (Third Discourse).
3. For a discussion of the subsequent development of 18th and 19th-century historiography after Richardson's pioneering work, see Watkin, op.cit., passim.
4. N. Taylor, 'Sir Albert Richardson: A Classic Case of Edwardianism', *Architectural Review*, 1966; reprinted in A. Service (ed.), *Edwardian Architecture and its Origins*, London, Architectural Press, 1975, pp.444–59.
5. For Richardson's early career and writings within the context of the revived interest in classical design and the formation of the Classical Society, see A. Powers, *Architectural Education in Britain, 1880–1914*, Ph.D. thesis, University of Cambridge, 1982, pp.168 ff.
6. Key articles by Richardson in the *Architectural Review* include 'The Style Neo-Grec' and 'The Empire Style in England – I–II', 1911, 'Karl Friedrich Schinkel' 1912, 'The Palais de Justice, Paris, and its remodelling by Joseph Louis Duc' 1913–1914, 'Jacques Ignace Hittorf', 1914, 'Jean Charles Krafft, Architecte-Dessinateur', 1914, 'Classic Architecture in Russia: I–IV' 1915–16. For detailed references, see list of writings.
7. A.E. Richardson and C. Lovett Gill, *London Houses from 1660 to 1820*, London, B.T. Batsford, 1911, p.vii.
8. C. Reilly, *Some Manchester Streets and Their Buildings*, Manchester, 1924, p.119.
9. A.E. Richardson, *Monumental Classic Architecture in Great Britain and Ireland during the Eighteenth and Nineteenth Centuries*, London, B.T. Batsford, 1914, p.vi.
10. Richardson took an active role in producing this impressive book and clearly influenced the design by Percy Delf Smith of the ornate gilt embossed cover which featured a motif based on a neo-Grec girandole, with a Greek fret border. The spine has a mask of Medusa. The superb photographs were specially taken by E. Dockree. See A. Crawford, 'In praise of collotype: Architectural illustration at the turn of the century', *Architectural History*, 25 (1982), pp.62–3, pl.G. The book's international distribution was handled by Charles Scribner's Sons, New York, for the United States, and C.F. Schulz & Co., Plauen, for Germany, Austria and Switzerland.
11. Richardson, op.cit., p.28. The phrase 'real architecture requires to be moulten in the imagination of the designer' is strikingly similar to Lutyens's image in a famous letter to Herbert Baker in 1903 where the former, referring to the handling of architecture, observed that: 'To the average man it is dry bones, but under the hand of Wren it glows and the stiff materials become as plastic clay' (C. Hussey, *The Life of Sir Edwin Lutyens*, 1950, London, Country Life, p.121).
12. Among the major London buildings alone, which were discussed and illustrated in *Monumental Classic Architecture*, the following were demolished: Dance's Newgate Prison (1902); Cockerell's Westminster Insurance Office, The Strand (1908); virtually all of Taylor's and Soane's Bank of England, apart from the screen walls (1921–37); Gibson's National Provincial Bank, Threadneedle Street (1922); Nash's Quadrant, Regent's Street (1923–28); almost the whole of the Adam brothers' Adelphi (1937); and Rennie's Waterloo Bridge (1937). Far later casualties were Hardwick's Euston Station Arch and Great Hall (1961) although Richardson did not live to see Cockerell's outstanding Sun Life Assurance Office, Threadneedle Street, destroyed in 1970.
13. Ibid., p.75.
14. Ibid. Reilly, as head of the School of Architecture at Liverpool, also promoted Cockerell's buildings as a subject for study at this time and had attempted to set up a 'Cockerell Prize' in 1910 (see Powers, op.cit., p.178).
15. 'The Academic in Architecture', *Journal of the Royal Institute of British Architects*, 3 ser., XIX, p.683.
16. John Summerson, Address on receiving the Royal Gold Medal in Architecture, *Journal of the Royal Institute of British Architects*, XII (1976), p.494.
17. A.E. Richardson and C. Lovett Gill, *Regional Architecture of the West of England*, London, Ernest Benn, 1924, p.ix.
18. S. Houfe, Sir A.E. Richardson Archive. 'An Assessment' (typescript), p.35. For a vivid portrait of Richardson's attitude towards collecting and the display of his historic possessions, see S.R. Houfe, *Sir Albert Richardson. The Professor*, Luton, White Crescent Press Ltd., 1980, especially Chapter 5, 'A Lifetime of Collecting'.
19. An early publication on this theme by Richardson was 'The Classic Tradition in America', *Architects' and Builders' Journal*, 21 January, 1914, pp.46.ff.
20. A.E. Richardson and H. Donaldson Eberlein, *The Smaller English House of the Later Renaissance 1660–1830*, London, B.T. Batsford, 1925, p.viii.
21. Ibid., p.185.

22. 'Modernism in Architecture', *Journal of the Royal Institute of British Architects*, June, 1928, p.518.
23. According to a communication from Simon Houfe, Richardson probably began collecting these drawings from about 1919, purchased from Batsford's antiquarian section. He is known to have acquired the album of C.J. Shopee, a minor architect/collector, in that year and inscribed in pencil on the cover 'many drawings added 1919–1926'. When the collection was divided at the close of the partnership with Gill in 1945 (having been purchased for the firm), many of the works were transferred to Ampthill. Gill's share appears to have included drawings of church interiors of the 1830s but is unlikely to have included any major works. A selection of Richardson's finest drawings were shown in two exhibitions in the 1960s, covered by the publications, *Compositions in Perspective. Designs by Noted Architects of the Past lent by Mrs Eric Houfe from the Collection of Sir Albert Richardson* (ed. S.R. Houfe), Cecil Higgins Gallery, Bedford, 1967; *Architectural Drawings from the Collection of Sir Albert Richardson* (ed. J. Wilton-Ely), University Galleries, Nottingham, and Newark-on-Trent Museum and Art Gallery, 1968. Certain key drawings also appeared in the later exhibition, *18th and 19th century British and Continental Architectural Drawings* (entries by C. Garcon and T. Landau, with introduction by H.M. Colvin), Clarendon Gallery, in association with Fischer Fine Art, London, 1984.
24. See sale catalogue, *Important Architectural Drawings and Watercolours: I. The Sir Albert Richardson Collection*, Christies, 30 November, 1983. The Mylne album was probably acquired prior to 1925 since the street elevation and ground-floor plan of The Wick, Richmond, is illustrated in *The Smaller English House* (fig.62), published that year.
25. A definitive monograph on Mylne is currently in preparation by Dr Roger Woodley, based on his doctoral thesis, University of London, 1999.
26. Both the Chambers letters and Goodchild Album are now in the collection of the RIBA.
27. D. Watkin, *The Life and Work of C.R. Cockerell*, London, A. Zwemmer, 1974, passim, especially pp.252–53 and pls.80, 134 and 144.
28. In 1948 Richardson edited an abridged reprint for Alec Tiranti of engravings from *Edifices de Rome Moderne* by Percier's student, Paul-Marie Letarouilly (1795–1855), based on the latter's meticulous survey of Renaissance classicism in Rome, made in 1821.
29. Richardson's articles of 1911 on 'The Empire Style in England' in *Architectural Review*, which extensively illustrated engravings of the Duchess Street interiors and furniture from Hope's Household Furniture, are referred to above in note 6. For his early acquisition of the pendant wall-lights attributed to Hope, probably from the Christie's 1917 sale, and the Regency Revival, see D. Watkin, *Thomas Hope and the Neo-Classical Idea, 1769–1831*, London, John Murray, 1968, pp.110, 191–2, 256–8. Richardson's writings and his furnished house with collections at Ampthill were also to have a considerable impact on the remarkable and evocative series of interiors created in his Rome apartment by the late Mario Praz who visited Ampthill and shared the same taste for the later Neo-Classical style, discussed in Praz's books, *The House of Life, Gusto Neoclassico* (Naples, 1959), and *An Illustrated History of Interior Decoration* (London, Thames & Hudson, 1964, originally published as *La filosophia dell'arredamento*).
30. Stevens was included among the neglected Victorian classicists in *Monumental Classic Architecture* with an illustration of the design for his first major commission, the bronze doors of Pennethorne's Geological Museum, Piccadilly, of 1846 (fig. 122).
31. A.E. Richardson, *The Old Inns of England*, London, 1934, p.v.
32. *English Taste in the Eighteenth Century from Baroque to neo-classic*, Royal Academy of Arts, London, 1955–56. Ever ready to promote an awareness of the lessons to be learnt from his favoured era, Richardson wrote in the Preface: 'It was an age of quality and elegance in which artists and craftsmen pursued a common ideal. The merit of the period was the intrinsic value of its artistic contributions to the world at large. Small wonder then that the Eighteenth Century has impressed modern life so completely with its tenets of good sense.'
33. *Southill. A Regency House*, London, Faber & Faber, 1951.
34. A.E. Richardson, *An Introduction to Georgian Architecture*, London, Art & Technics, 1949, p.96.
35. Ibid., pp.127–28.

SOME MEMORIES PAGES 23–26

1. This memoir was written in 1966 at the request of Simon Houfe, and printed here by his kind permission.
2. This is incorrect. Reilly was Professor of Architecture at Liverpool 1904–1933, Adshead was Professor of Civic Design at Liverpool, 1909–1914, and Professor of Town Planning at University College, London, 1914–35.
3. Hanslip Fletcher's work appeared mostly in the *Sunday Times*.

A DISCRIMINATING TASTE PAGES 27–39

1. 'Sketches From Memory' by an inconspicuous American. Unpublished typescript, c.1955.
2. A.E. Richardson's diary, 22nd October 1949.
3. Still in the possession of the family.
4. Ibid.
5. Ibid.
6. *Examples of Old Furniture English and Foreign, Drawn and Described* by Alfred Ernest Chancellor (Batsford), London 1898.
7. Undated cutting in scrap-book.
8. 'Present Day Tendencies in Internal Decorative Work', *The Estate Magazine*, no date.
9. 'Richard Phené Spiers, Architect and Archaeologist', by A.T. Bolton, *Architectural Review*, Nov 1916, pp.96–100.
10. *Architectural Review*, November, p.255; December 1911, p.315.
11. Ibid., November.
12. Ibid., December.
13. Created with this by the late Clifford Musgrave.
14. *The Estate Magazine*, no date.
15. Letter to the author from W. Angell, 1966.
16. 'The Arts and Crafts Exhibition,' RIBA *Journal*, Vol.24, 3rd series, 11 Nov 1916, pp.9–12.
17. Kathleen Richardson *Moving In*, 1985, p.1.
18. A holiday at Wood End, Bolnhurst in 1907.
19. The re-instatement of panelling at Chillingham Castle, 1942 and the incorporation of Admiral Russell's staircase at South Walsham Hall, 1960.
20. *Homes & Gardens*, June 1924, pp.21–23.
21. *Country Life*, 22 December 1922, p.747.
22. John Cornforth, *The Search For A Style, Country Life Architecture 1897–1935*, 1988, p.57.
23. The Professor of English Literature at Rome, *The House of Life*, 1964, pp.314–5.
24. These were mostly dispersed in a sale, Christie's, Wednesday 30 November 1983.
25. *Country Life*, 8 December 1934.
26. *Country Life*, 1 October 1927.
27. Memoir by T.R. Henn at Ampthill.
28. James Lees-Milne, *Prophesying Peace*, 1977, p.224.
29. Robert Wraight, 'A Genteel Mission to Sir Albert', *The Tatler*, 15 November 1961, p.472.
30. Simon Houfe, *Sir Albert Richardson The Professor*, 1980, pp.218–9.

ALBERT RICHARDSON: A CRITICAL SURVEY PAGES 41–71

1. 'The Harding Interview', BBC Home Service, 9 December, 1954, transcript courtesy of BBC Written Archives Centre.
2. RIBA *Journal*, LIV, May 1947, p.357, where Davis attributes it to Richardson. A variant is given in Richardson's obituary by G.J. Howling in *Builder*, 7 February, 1964, p.273, where it is attributed to Stanley Adshead's partner, S.C. Ramsey.
3. Karel Honzik, 'England's part in the modern architecture', *Stavba* (Prague), XIV, Spring 1937, p.57.
4. Richardson 'The Academic in Architecture', RIBA Journal, XIX, 1912, p.683
5. Richardson and Gill, *London Houses 1660–1820*, 1911, p.2.
6. C.H. Reilly, 'London Streets and their buildings – XI', *Country Life*, 17 January, 1925, pp.103–4.
7. *Architects' Journal*, 23 January, 1924, p.192.
8. 'The Modern Movement in Architecture', lecture at Manchester University, *Builder*, 29 February, 1924, p.342. A more extensive and polished version of the text was printed in RIBA *Journal*, Series III, XXXI, 1924, pp.267–74.
9. C.H. Reilly "The Year's Work', *Architects' Journal*, 5 Jan, 1927, p.22.
10. W.R. Lethaby to A.E. Richardson, 29 February 1926, collection Simon Houfe.
11. 'Modern Street Architecture' Lecture to the London Society, *Builder*, 6 May, 1927, p.739.
12. *Architects' Journal*, 30 November, 1932, p.689.
13. Richardson and Corfiato, *Design in Civil Architecture*, Vol.1, Elevational Treatments, London, The English University Presses Ltd., 1948, p.21.
14. Ian Nairn, *Modern Buildings in London*, London, London Transport, 1964, p.2.
15. Sir John Summerson, letter to Gavin Stamp, 29 August 1986, courtesy of Gavin Stamp.
16. Nairn, op.cit., p.81.
17. Pevsner, *Buildings of England, Bedfordshire, Huntingdon and Peterborough*, Harmondsworth, Penguin Books, 1968.
18. 'Frankly Speaking' Richardson interviewed by John Betjeman and Margaret Lane, Home Service, 15 May, 1956. BBC Written Archives, Caversham.
19. I am grateful to Peter Smithson for a discussion of this episode in his career on 29 June 1999.
20. Gordon E. Cherry & Leith Penny, *Holford, a study in architecture, planning and civic design*, London, Mansell 1986, p.161.
21. 'At Home and Abroad', Home Service, 11 March, 1955.
22. Quoted ibid., p.165.
23. Thomas Sharp, *Town and Countryside*, London, Oxford University Press, 1932, p.217.
24. Nikolaus Pevsner, *The Buildings of England, Bedfordshire, Huntingdon and Peterborough*, Harmondsworth, Penguin Books, 1968, p.38.
25. 'The Gentle Art of Making Enemies', *Building*, XXV, August, p.305.
26. Susan Buck-Morss, *The Dialectics of Seeing*, 1989, Cambridge, Mass & London, MIT Press, p.74.

PHOTOGRAPHIC CREDITS

Bedfordshire Record Office (items on deposit by Simon Houfe, all photos by Richard Ivey): figures 41, 42, 45, 47, 49, 50, 53, 62, 63, 64, 66, 71, 72, 73, 74, 88, 89, 90, 97, 101, 102, 103, 104, 105, 106, 114

Simon Houfe, cover, figures 1, 2, 7, 8, 14, 18, 24, 26, 27, 28, 29, 31, 32, 33, 34, 35, 36, 37, 39, 40, 43, 46, 48, 51, 52, 54, 55, 56, 60, 61, 65, 67, 68, 69, 75, 76, 77, 78, 79, 80, 83, 92, 94, 95, 96, 98, 99, 100, 108, 109, 110, 111, 112, 113, 115

British Architectural Library: figures 44, 57, 81, 82, 84, 85

English Heritage Photo Library: figure 70

Michael Manni Photographic, Cambridge, courtesy of Gonville & Caius College: figure 25

Alan Powers: figures 38, 58, 91, 107

Peter Smithson: figures 86, 87

Denny Wickham: figure 93

figure 115
Albert Richardson, drawn by Hanslip Fletcher, 1918